Toni Morrison's

Paradise

Text by
David M. Gracer
(M.A., University of Wyoming)

Illustrations by
Karen Pica

Research & Education Association
Dr. M. Fogiel, Director

MAXnotes® for
PARADISE

Printed in the United States of America

Library of Congress Catalog Card Number 99-74132

International Standard Book Number 0-87891-198-7

MAXnotes® is a registered trademark of
Research & Education Association, Piscataway, New Jersey 08854

What **MAXnotes**® *Will Do for You*

This book is intended to help you absorb the essential contents and features of Toni Morrison's *Paradise* and to help you gain a thorough understanding of the work. The book has been designed to do this more quickly and effectively than any other study guide.

For best results, this **MAXnotes** book should be used as a companion to the actual work, not instead of it. The interaction between the two will greatly benefit you.

To help you in your studies, this book presents the most up-to-date interpretations of every section of the actual work, followed by questions and fully explained answers that will enable you to analyze the material critically. The questions also will help you to test your understanding of the work and will prepare you for discussions and exams.

Meaningful illustrations are included to further enhance your understanding and enjoyment of the literary work. The illustrations are designed to place you into the mood and spirit of the work's settings.

The **MAXnotes** also include summaries, character lists, explanations of plot, and section-by-section analyses. A biography of the author and discussion of the work's historical context will help you put this literary piece into the proper perspective of what is taking place.

The use of this study guide will save you the hours of preparation time that would ordinarily be required to arrive at a complete grasp of this work of literature. You will be well-prepared for classroom discussions, homework, and exams. The guidelines that are included for writing papers and reports on various topics will prepare you for any added work which may be assigned.

The **MAXnotes** will take your grades "to the max."

Dr. Max Fogiel
Program Director

Contents

**Each chapter includes List of Characters, Summary,
Analysis, Study Questions and Answers, and
Suggested Essay Topics.**

MAXnotes® are simply the best – but don't just take our word for it...

"... I have told every bookstore in the area to carry your MAXnotes. They are the only notes I recommend to my students. There is no comparison between MAXnotes and all other notes ..."
– High School Teacher & Reading Specialist,
Arlington High School, Arlington, MA

"... I discovered the MAXnotes when a friend loaned me her copy of the MAXnotes for Romeo and Juliet. The book really helped me understand the story. Please send me a list of stores in my area that carry the MAXnotes. I would like to use more of them ..."
– Student, San Marino, CA

"... The two MAXnotes titles that I have used have been very, very useful in helping me understand the subject matter reviewed. Thank you for creating the MAXnotes series ..."
– Student, Morrisville, PA

A Glance at Some of the Characters

Mavis Albright

Connie

Gigi (Grace)

K. D.

Arnette Fleetwood

Dovey Morgan

Zechariah Morgan

Patricia Best

Introduction

The Life and Work of Toni Morrison

Toni Morrison was born Chloe Anthony Wofford on February 18, 1931, to George and Ramah Willis Wofford in Lorain, Ohio. Although life in a post-depression steel-mill town would have been difficult for most children, Chloe, the second of four children, had loving and strong-willed parents. They taught her much about how to heal the wounds caused by racism.

Morrison graduated from Howard University in 1953. It was during her college years that she adopted what had been her nickname, Toni, which she'd taken from her middle name. In 1955, she received her M.A. in English from Cornell, and for the next two years, she taught English at Texas Southern University, then returned to teach at Howard. She married Harold Morrison, a Jamaican architect; their first son, Harold Ford, was born in 1962. A second son, Slade Kevin, was born in 1966. After divorcing Morrison, Toni left teaching to work at Random House, a publishing company in Syracuse, New York. She worked there for the next 20 years, and during the same time period, she taught and lectured at several colleges, wrote and published novels, and raised her two sons.

Toni Morrison's first novel, *The Bluest Eye* (1970), was very well received in both popular and critical circles. Since then she has published six more novels: *Sula* (1974), *Song of Solomon* (1977), *Tar Baby* (1981), *Beloved* (1987), *Jazz* (1992), and *Paradise* (1998). She has also published a play, *Dreaming Emmett* (1986), and a collection of essays, *Playing in the Dark* (1991).

Morrison joined the faculty of Princeton University in 1989; she was the first African-American woman to receive a chaired position at an Ivy League university. In addition to the Nobel Prize for Literature, Toni Morrison won the Pulitzer Prize in 1986 and the National Book Critics Circle Award for *Song of Solomon* in 1977.

Historical Background

Paradise is set in a small town in Oklahoma and shows how a community's past can influence, and perhaps determine, its present and future. As with Morrison's two previous novels, *Beloved* and *Jazz*, *Paradise* is based on thorough research into a period of African-American history.

There is a rich history of African Americans in the American West, and although this subject was left out of many of the history books used in most classrooms, this is now starting to change. Some people fled the policies of slavery, whereas others simply sought opportunity in less-populated parts of the country. There were many good reasons for blacks to flee the South, before, during, and after the Civil War. Advertising, recruitment campaigns, and land incentives ensured that many thousands of black settlers went West, ready for new lives that would involve greater freedom and control of their own destinies.

All-black towns sprang up by the dozens throughout Oklahoma, Kansas, and elsewhere. Some of the towns were quite large. Two in particular seem to be the inspiration for material in *Paradise*. The town of Boley, Oklahoma boasted 4,000 citizens. When Booker T. Washington visited Boley in 1905, he was impressed with what he found; there had not been an arrest in Boley for two years (compare this fact to an observation in *Paradise*'s first chapter: "It neither had nor needed a jail.") Langston City, also in Oklahoma, was considerably larger and had its own newspaper, which, not surprisingly, concerned itself with issues affecting the town. Although all settlers, regardless of race, were of great importance to the town, the town had to make sure that each and every one of its citizens would pull his or her own weight.

Of all the virtues for which the American West was famous, the most important was self-sufficiency. No town could afford to receive several hundred poor, broken refugees from the South.

Moreover, as a general principle, weakness was not tolerated. Hence, the newspapers issued in black towns were strident in their demands that newcomers not be a burden. The *Langston City Herald* exhorted black settlers coming to Oklahoma from other parts of the country, "Come Prepared or Not at All." This sentiment greatly disheartens the novel's characters when they read it on their way to found Haven. Both Boley and Langston City are specifically mentioned in *Paradise*. These towns had to endure a variety of pressures and destructive elements. While white settlers in the region did not enjoy their neighbors, Native Americans saw all settlers as threats. *Paradise* is the story of how the people in the fictional town of Ruby, Oklahoma, dealt with those pressures.

Master List of Characters

Nine Unnamed Men from the town of Ruby—*they are the figures around whom Chapter One centers.*

Morgan—*the ironmonger (blacksmith) who contributes his nails to the Oven at the founding of the town of Haven.*

Ossie—*a citizen of Haven who had once organized a horse race as part of a town celebration and picnic.*

Ruby—*the woman after whom the town of Ruby was named. She was the mother of the youngest of the nine men, the aunt of the twins.*

Mavis Albright—*a housewife in Maryland whose baby twins have suffocated in a parked car; she is 27 years old.*

Frank Albright—*Mavis' husband.*

Sal—*Mavis and Frank's daughter, the eldest of their children.*

Frankie and **Billy James**—*Mavis and Frank's two sons.*

Merle and **Pearl**—*Mavis and Frank's deceased twins.*

June—*the journalist who interviews Mavis and her children.*

Birdie Goodroe—*Mavis' mother.*

Dusty—*the first of the hitchhikers Mavis picks up on her way West.*

Bennie—*the last of the hitchhikers that Mavis picks up.*

Connie—*a woman who takes Mavis in at the Convent. Connie reappears as Consolata later in the novel.*

Soane Morgan (nee **Blackhorse**)—*a rather formal, well-to-do woman who comes to the Convent to pick up pecans and some other mystery item. She is married to Deacon Morgan.*

Soane Morgan's son—*an unnamed young man who gives Mavis a ride to the local gas station.*

Mother—*a very old woman in the Convent who seems to be one of the former nuns. Her full name is Mary Magna.*

Gigi (Grace)—*an outsider who comes to Ruby and goes to the Convent.*

K. D.—*The nephew of Deek and Steward Morgan, and the nephew written about in the first chapter.*

Good and **Ben**—*the two dogs K. D. tends.*

Arnette Fleetwood—*a young woman who has been keeping company with K. D. She is fifteen and pregnant.*

Billie Delia—*Arnette's friend.*

Deacon (Deek) Morgan—*the more reserved and subtle of the two Morgan brothers.*

Steward Morgan—*the more outspoken of the two Morgan brothers.*

Arnold Fleetwood—*Arnette's father, and one of the leading men in Haven.*

Mabel Fleetwood—*Arnold's wife, a woman whose people played an important role in the histories of both Haven and Ruby.*

Jeff Fleetwood—*Arnold's son and Arnette's brother. Jeff and his wife, Sweetie, live with his parents.*

Sweetie Fleetwood—*Jeff's wife.*

Reverend Misner—*the town's main spiritual leader.*

Mikey—*a boyfriend from Gigi's past.*

Dice—*the man on the train who tells Gigi about a strange landmark outside of Ruby.*

Roger Best—*the man who gives Gigi a ride to the Convent. Frustrated in his hopes to become a doctor, he became an undertaker.*

Dovey Morgan (nee **Blackhorse**)—*wife of Steward Morgan and sister of Soane Morgan.*

Menus Jury—*a man who lives in Ruby; a member of one of the founding families. He served in Vietnam and has a drinking problem.*

Reverend Pulliam—*one of Ruby's three spiritual leaders. The reverend of New Zion (Methodist) Church, he represents the old ways of thinking and decries the behavior of the youth in Ruby.*

Destry Beauchamp—*a young man who speaks up at the town meeting.*

The Friend—*a mysterious but friendly man who visits Dovey Morgan on the porch of their little house in town. Neither Dovey nor the reader ever learns much about him.*

Elder Morgan—*the older brother of Steward and Deacon. He does not appear in the novel, but remains a figure in the memories of the twins.*

Rector Morgan (**Big Daddy**)—*the father of Elder, Steward, Deacon, and (the late) Ruby Morgan. Like his father, Zechariah, Rector remains a figure in the memories of the twins, and is featured in the stories/history lessons told by the invisible narrator.*

Zechariah Morgan (**Big Papa**)—*Rector Morgan's father and one of the founders of the town of Haven. He is a shadowy, almost mythical figure, because there are few clear memories of just what kind of man he was. Zechariah was an ironmonger, and put the message on the Oven's door.*

Anna Flood—*the proprietor of Flood's General Store. The daughter of Ace Flood. She is in love with Reverend Richard Misner.*

Seneca—*a young woman who is wandering aimlessly. Abandoned when she was five, Seneca is meek and very accommodating to others.*

Jean—*Seneca's sister, who abandoned Seneca.*

Eddie Turtle—*the young man with whom Seneca becomes involved. He is serving a six-month sentence in jail, and Seneca brings him a Bible.*

Mrs. Turtle—*Eddie's mother, whom Seneca visits in Wichita, Kansas.*

Norma Fox—*a mysterious woman who "hires" Seneca for some private services.*

David—*Norma's chauffeur, who approaches Seneca about employment.*

Leon Fox—*Norma's husband.*

Pallas Truelove—*a young woman with a troubled past. She seems to be a child from an interracial marriage. Originally from Los Angeles, she runs away from home and eventually finds the Convent.*

Carlos—*Pallas' boyfriend. He was the janitor at the exclusive girls' school she attended. He is considerably older than Pallas and eventually leaves her for her mother.*

Patricia Best—*mother of Billie Delia and daughter of Roger and Delia Best; she is a schoolteacher.*

Nathan DuPres—*the oldest man in town. He tells a story from his childhood at the Christmas production.*

Sister Roberta—*one of the nuns at the Native American girls' school.*

Penny and **Clarissa**—*two Native American girls who look up to Connie and appeal to her for help.*

Lone DuPres—*Ruby's midwife, and one of the town's oldest women. She helps Connie to explore and develop her abilities.*

Piedade—*a mythical figure in Consolata's stories and lessons. Though described as a woman, Piedade has various powers and may be something of a shape-shifter.*

Save-Marie—*The youngest of Jeff and Sweetie Fleetwood's sickly children. The other children were Noah, Esther, and Ming. Her death is the first death inside the town of Ruby.*

Manley Gibson—*Gigi's father, a convict recently removed from death row.*

Dee Dee Truelove—*Pallas' mother*

Summary of the Novel

Paradise is about the relationship between two communities—the town of Ruby, Oklahoma, and a very small but largely self-sufficient group of women who live in what has come to be known as the Convent, located on the outskirts of Ruby.

The people of Ruby were once filled with a common purpose—they trusted, needed, and relied upon each other. But in more recent times, with which this novel is concerned, Ruby has been experiencing a whole range of difficulties. The town's shared existence is threatened, and in their desperation to find some kind of solution, the townspeople blame and attack the women in the Convent. The women become convenient scapegoats for all the unresolved emotions pent up in the prominent men of Ruby, who have felt powerless to halt the unraveling of their homes.

Paradise is a novel of interwoven portraits. They are not exactly portraits of people, places, or of periods of time; they are portraits of striving and conflict. The portraits center on all of the things that are done to protect what has been worked for and sacrificed for, to keep the town safe from the forces of destruction that lie in wait all around.

The events of the first chapter actually occur near the end of the chronological story. The year is 1976, and a few men from Ruby attack the women who live in a single building, which is referred to as "the Convent," not very far from their town. The men believe (or at least they tell themselves) that they are committing this act in order to protect their way of life. The specific threat that the women represent is not fully explained at first, but that doesn't matter for the moment—what matters is action. After the smoke of the violence clears, the reader is taken on a tour of the lives that made up both the town of Ruby and the Convent, a place where a few women have come together to try to help one another.

The rest of the novel jumps back and forth in time, partially because of the characters' memories and partially due to the omniscient narrator's subtle voice, which feeds the reader bits and pieces of the larger story. Ultimately, the explanation of the raid comes out of everything that led to the raid. The story of the town's history is built up slowly, and we start to understand why the men of Ruby are the way they are.

The town of Ruby was founded in 1950 by a group of African Americans, many of them recently returned from World War II. Ruby was born from the relic of another town, named Haven, which was also in Oklahoma. Haven was founded in 1890 by black settlers (the parents and grandparents of the men who founded Ruby) who had arrived there from Mississippi and Louisiana. Many of those settlers had important careers and were very accomplished, but various racist forces had come together, causing these people to seek a better life for themselves and their families. On the way from these southern states, the settlers endured many hardships; the worst of these misfortunes took place in Fairly, Oklahoma.

Many of the residents of Ruby once lived in Haven, and that town had a rich, vibrant life from 1890 to the late 1940s, by which time the town had no future. The trials and hardships of 80 years have shaped the residents' sense of determination about who they are and how to protect what is important to them.

Seventeen miles away from Ruby is a single building surrounded by plains and rolling hills. It is called "The Convent," because it was once a Catholic school run by nuns. The nuns have left, and the building has a newer story. A woman named Connie, who has spent most of her life with the nuns and who once ran the school, takes in women whom have left society: an ill-fated housewife hounded by her own family; an independent young woman, uninterested in someone else's imposed ideas of morality, judged as a threat to the community; and two young women who have been traumatized by events in their lives.

The Convent becomes their home, and it is like a paradise for them. But their lives come into conflict with the people of Ruby, and the ultimate manifestation of that conflict is brutal violence. One message the reader can take from this is that paradise has to be fought for in order to be achieved, and once it has been won, it will have to be protected by further fighting.

At times, it seems that *Paradise* consists of several large, intertwined stories, and some of these stories stand opposite each other. The novel is a demandingly historical work, and the reader is confronted by a great amount of hard data, such as family trees and historical facts. At the same time, however, the novel contains increasing amounts of mysticism. Different readers will respond to and interpret these parts of the novel in different ways, but a combination of careful reading, logic, and suspension of disbelief will lead the reader to some clear conclusions. The novel ends with glimpses into fantastical worlds, which one cannot hope to understand if one insists on using logic alone.

Estimated Reading Time

The average reading time for this 318 page novel is about 12–15 hours, or approximately one to three hours for each chapter. But reading this novel will require more than just time. *Paradise* is a formidable novel, and it will challenge most readers. For example, stories begun early in the novel will not be completed or explained until the end of the novel.

Paradise also gives the impression that one is reading history—albeit a history filtered through the idiosyncratic style of a storyteller who does not want to give us all the information at once but wants to make us work for the understanding we receive. Morrison makes her readers work. Teachers using this book in a course will probably want to examine the novel with students one chapter at a time in order to ensure that the students are following the difficult narrative scheme and presentation of characters.

Paradise

Chapter One: Ruby

New Characters:

Nine Unnamed Men from the town of Ruby: *they are the figures around whom this chapter centers. The reader learns the following information about them:*

- The men are not hurrying or acting in a nervous fashion.

- Several of the men are related: there is a father-and-son team and a pair of twin brothers.

- The twin brothers are 52 years old. They are not very much alike; in fact, now that they are grown men, they no longer even look alike. One is a natural leader who heads this expedition. The brothers are grandchildren of Morgan, one of the founders of Haven, who put the message on the Oven door. They are the brothers of Ruby; it was her death that settled the debate about the town's name.

- The youngest of the men is a nephew of the twin brothers. He is troubled by mental pictures of the murdered victims. He thinks that one of them is staring and waving her fingers at him. He won a local horse race in Haven when he was just a boy. Ruby was his mother, and he grew up spoiled by sympathetic elders.

Morgan: *the ironmonger (blacksmith) who contributes his nails to the Oven, at the founding of Haven. We find that this must be his last name, but we do not learn what his first name is.*

Ossie: *a citizen of Haven who had once organized a horse race as part of a town celebration and picnic. We find out later that his last name is Beauchamp.*

Ruby: *the woman after whom the town of Ruby was named. She was the mother of the youngest of the nine men, the aunt of the twins.*

Summary

The chapter describes a search conducted by nine armed men, in Oklahoma on a cold, early morning in July. They have already shot one woman and are seeking the others. They move through the single building known as "the Convent" slowly and carefully, as if they are on a military mission, or as if they are hunting. They have a definite strategy, separating into pairs so as to search the building systematically. The women who currently live in the Convent are not nuns.

The Convent's history is explained. Once the showy home of an embezzler, the building's many original gaudy ornaments and fixtures were either removed or broken off by the nuns who had taken it over. Larger items, such as bathtubs, remain.

As the pairs of men search the rooms, they keep expecting to find evidence of crimes and unnatural behavior. They suspect that horrible, unacceptable things have been going on in this house; their suspicions are alluded to throughout the chapter. What they find is enough to disturb and disgust them: candles on the floor and strange figurines, slimy plates and lack of order, some blood and filth.

The writing jumps back and forth between the activities of the men in the present and stories of their past, which come out of the histories of two towns: Haven and Ruby. The men are from Ruby, but in this chapter we learn far more about Haven, which grew, thrived, and was dying when people there decided to start again and drove to found and build their new town, Ruby.

Haven was founded by 15 families in 1890. The founders, the Old Fathers, suffered many misfortunes and humiliations when they came to Oklahoma from Mississippi and Louisiana to make a home. This made them tough, proud, and distrustful of all outsiders. These are sentiments that the New Fathers kept with them when they founded Ruby. The first thing built in Haven was a huge Oven, which became the center and the physical embodiment of the town. Every brick of the Oven seemed perfect, and the door was a thick, heavy piece of iron, containing a special message made of welded nails. Meat, especially game meat, was cooked to perfection in the Oven over low flames.

Haven had a thousand citizens in 1905, but only 500 in 1934. Eventually the population dropped to 80. Eighteen stubborn people remained at the very end. In 1950, nine families gave up on Haven and moved 240 miles west to Ruby. Haven's Oven was carefully broken up and reassembled in the new town. The families settled on land they'd bought together from their military discharge pay. Life was better again, but now, more than 25 years after the move, they perceive a new threat.

The chapter ends by completing a circle. The men who approached the Convent in the waist-high mist at five in the morning are now prepared to do what they feel they must do. Having searched the building, the men meet and see three women running toward the rising sun. The men take aim and fire; although the reader is not told what follows, it seems unlikely that the women escape.

Analysis

At only 16 pages, Ruby is one of the shorter "chapters" of this novel. Yet notice that even in such a small space, Morrison is telling several stories at once. These tales are related by the foundation of history: cause and effect.

This short chapter may seem long because Morrison does not provide the reader with an exposition, or introduction, to the story or the characters. There is an enormous amount of mystery here. The techniques used in this novel tend to increase the amount of mystery, because Morrison tells only part of a story at any one time.

Readers who are unhappy about the way that Morrison with-holds or hides information might do well to picture themselves sitting next to someone who is part historian, part great storyteller. When in that situation, one must strain to catch every detail, be-cause one never knows when the seemingly smallest thing will be important later on. A reader can go back a few pages or chapters and check the story; this is a luxury listeners don't have.

For example, the reader would do well to remember, among many other things, the list of incidents that have so disturbed the men: "A mother was knocked down the stairs by her cold-eyed daughter. Four damaged infants were born into one family. Daugh-ters refused to get out of bed. Brides disappeared on their honey-moons." These stories will be finished later.

Although the reader will probably wonder who these men are, the reader's biggest question might well be, "Why are they doing this?" In most books we read or movies we see, we sympathize with characters by understanding why they behave the way they do and learning what their motives are. In *Paradise*, the reader is not given the motive in a clear fashion, and this may be frustrating, espe-cially because we are reading about armed men hunting and shoot-ing down unarmed women.

Could there be justifiable cause for such a massacre? The main job of this novel will be to answer this question, but not all at once. Morrison will serve us very small pieces of the answer, one by one, never giving us much at one time. The reader is obliged to play detective. Time after time, connections between characters and events are hinted at, but not confirmed or explained until many, many pages later. For the moment, the omniscient narrator indi-cates that the Convent represents a threat to the community of Ruby. Strange rumors are circulating about what goes on there, and events occur that are thought to be linked to the Convent: disap-pearances, unexplainable deaths, and other bizarre happenings and problems.

Perhaps the men have a good reason, or several good reasons, for doing what they are doing. The stories about Haven and the individual men, from how they served their country in World War II to how they now have families, show that the men have a sense of honor and responsibility. Morrison's decision to leave the men

unnamed gives an impersonal impression, as if the men's identities are unimportant, as if they are merely an anonymous mob. But some of the men will become important characters later in the novel.

Although the reason for the raid is not spelled out in this chapter, it seems that the people of Ruby have a combination of fears, including prostitution and the fall of morals, child abuse, murder, and the possibility of Satanism. Consider this chapter as a response to a problem—not, to be sure, a very pleasant response, and one that might well have consequences for the killers. But it's still a response. The job of the rest of the novel will be to show us the problem and thereby put this response in context.

As we read the novel, we can understand the motives behind the act. We might even sympathize with the men, but not for simple reasons. The fact is that vast mysteries surround us here in the first chapter, and much remains to be explained. Though we learn about some of the armed men throughout the chapter, especially the twin brothers (they were born in Haven in 1924, enlisted in the army in 1942, and married in 1949), there is so much that has been left out.

From the very first sentence, the reader is plunged into the detailed perceptions and actions of the unnamed men. Their observations of the lights, colors, objects, and rooms of the building they are searching make the reader sense that they are doing something dangerous.

The language is sophisticated and beautiful. We are shown vivid details of the Convent's rooms and get real insight into the men, despite the fact that we do not know their names. The strength of the story and the writing itself make us willing to wait for a more detailed explanation. The descriptive language has another interesting aspect; it might well serve to make the men's endeavor less evil. It gives the reader the impression that they are not common murderers or even criminals of any kind. They act as if they are on an important mission, whose end justifies the violent means they employ. This is indicated in the second paragraph, where we read "…the women they are obliged to stampede or kill…." The men of Ruby feel that they have a sacred duty to protect their town.

Study Questions

1. How far is the Convent from Ruby, and how far is Ruby from the nearest town?

2. How many women are in the Convent?

3. What are the names taped above two of the bedroom doors?

4. What is one thing that the women who currently live in the Convent have in common with the nuns who once lived there?

5. What was the message on the iron door of the Oven?

6. How many horses entered the race that Ossie organized and did they all run?

7. What medal decorated the ribbon for the winner of the race?

8. Who awarded the medal to the winner of the race?

9. What did the veterans want to name the new town?

10. How long did the settlers call their new town New Haven?

Answers

1. The Convent is seventeen miles from Ruby, and Ruby is 90 miles from any other town.

2. It seems that there are no more than four women in the Convent. We know this because there are nine men, and we are told that the nine men are more than twice the number of the women.

3. The names taped above two of the bedroom doors are "Seneca" and "Divine."

4. The women who live in the Convent now, like the nuns before them, sell the produce and barbecue sauce they grow and make.

5. The message on the iron door of the Oven is not revealed in the first chapter.

6. Ten horses entered the race that Ossie organized, but only three horses actually ran.

7. Ossie's Purple Heart decorated the ribbon for the winner of the race.

8. The little girl with the most poppies in her hair awarded the medal to the winner of the race.

9. The veterans wanted to name the new town after the battles they were in. Those who fought in the Pacific theater suggested Guam or Inchon, whereas the ones who fought in Europe wanted names from their battlefields.

10. The settlers called their new town New Haven for three years.

Suggested Essay Topics

1. What specific details most made an impression on you? Which details seemed to communicate a mood?

2. Try to describe the personalities, beliefs, and histories of the men, based on the descriptions of them in this chapter. In particular, explore their feelings about what they are doing. Hints and indications of their feelings can be found throughout the chapter.

Chapter Two: Mavis

New Characters:

Mavis Albright: *a housewife in Maryland whose baby twins have suffocated in a parked car; she is 27 years old.*

Frank Albright: *Mavis' husband.*

Sal: *Mavis and Frank's daughter, the eldest of their children. She repeatedly hurts her mother in a most malicious and obvious fashion.*

Frankie James: *one of Mavis and Frank's two sons.*

Billy James: *the other of Mavis and Frank's two sons.*

Merle and **Pearl:** *the twin babies whose deaths begin the chapter.*

June: *The journalist who interviews Mavis and her children; her* *supposedly professional probing seems condescending and unkind.*

Birdie Goodroe: *Mavis' mother. She allows Mavis to stay with her, but is not supportive of and does not really trust her daughter. After several days, Birdie calls Frank to come and get his wife.*

Dusty: *the first of the hitchhikers Mavis picks up on her way West.*

Bennie: *the last of the hitchhikers that Mavis picks up. Bennie sings very well and is Mavis' favorite, even though Bennie steals Mavis' raincoat and yellow boots.*

Connie: *an unusual woman who takes Mavis in at the Convent.*

Soane Morgan (nee **Blackhorse**): *a rather formal, well-to-do woman who comes to the Convent to pick up pecans and some other mystery item. She gives Mavis a ride from the Convent. She is married to Deacon Morgan.*

Soane Morgan's son: *an unnamed young man who gives Mavis a ride to the local gas station. Though we do not learn his name, we know that he and his brother are not the twin brothers from the first chapter, because he is too young.*

Mother: *a very old woman in the Convent, who seems to be one of the former nuns. She is cared for by Connie. Although not strong physically, she has a remarkable presence. Her name is Mary Magna.*

Summary

This chapter centers around Mavis Albright, who, at the beginning of the chapter, is living in Maryland in 1968. She is enduring a horrific crisis; her twin babies are dead, and reporters and photographers are prying into what should be her private grief. The reporters' inconsiderate questions and insinuations do not bother Mavis much, because she has more pressing concerns. Mavis is afraid of her family. Sal, Mavis and Frank's eldest child, goes out of her way to hurt her mother, pinching her (viciously enough to draw blood) and stomping on her feet. These injuries feed Mavis' fears that her family is plotting to do her serious harm, perhaps even kill her. Her husband and children seem to be communicating their own agendas, without including her in their secrets. She feels surrounded by danger.

In the middle of the night, Mavis steals Frank's car and manages to flee her family. She maneuvers as silently as possible in the dark, fearing discovery and attack. After stopping briefly at an acquaintance's house, Mavis goes to her mother, Birdie Goodroe. She lives at her mother's for less than a week, planning her departure, then suddenly leaves when she overhears Birdie tell Frank to come and get Mavis. Mavis gets the car painted and heads West, toward California. As her money diminishes, she picks up hitchhikers to help with gasoline expenses. Girls seem safer than men. A pair of hitchers asks Mavis to drop them in a cemetery, where various people, including soldiers, walk around as if they are in a park. The last of the hitchers is Bennie, with whom Mavis forms a brief friendship. Bennie's singing comforts Mavis, and Bennie's sudden disappearance (with Mavis' raincoat and boots) depresses her. At one point, Mavis is sure that she sees Frank, her husband, at a gas station. The fact that the man's hair and clothes are different from Frank's does not shake her conviction that she was almost captured.

Running out of gas at last, Mavis suffers some indecision before leaving the car. She happens to find the Convent, where she meets Connie, a woman who works and perhaps lives there. Despite an initial awkwardness, the two women get along and begin to talk easily. Connie offers to go to California with Mavis, but that seems to be a joke. Connie feeds Mavis and asks her to help a little by shelling pecans. Significantly, the building seems to have strange echoes and presences for Mavis. From her first few minutes at the Convent, she senses that children are near. The perception disturbs her slightly.

While Connie and Mavis are conversing, a visitor arrives—Soane Morgan, who lives in Ruby but is clearly comfortable at the Convent. She and Connie talk. Soane is here to pick something up, but the reader never learns what the item is. She agrees to give Mavis a lift to the gas station, where the latter, after some difficulty with the gas station attendant, gets a gas can. Along the way, a radio station is playing old Motown songs, good music according to Mavis. Soane's son gives Mavis a ride back to her car. Because it's dark, Mavis decides to return to the Convent. She never gets to California, preferring life in this new place.

Later, Mavis meets Mother, who knows the history of the Convent and speaks Latin. Mother is attended to by Connie; the two seem to be somewhat at odds. The first meeting between Mavis and Mother makes a definite impression on Mavis, who feels at home in the Convent. She is there years later, in 1976, when the men arrive with guns in the early morning, as described in the first chapter.

Analysis

Although it starts with what seems like a completely unconnected story, this chapter ties in with the first one. None of the members of Mavis' family are true characters in this chapter; they are not fleshed out and have no individual traits. They exist only to illustrate the kind of life from which Mavis had to escape. For although Mavis must bear some of the responsibility for the twins' deaths, the callous way in which she was treated by the rest of the family contributed to their demise as well. We can see that, whether or not there is any basis to Mavis' fears about her family's intentions to do her harm, she is trapped in a horrible situation. Her family does not really communicate, and so none of them is really safe. Perhaps the family isn't really trying to kill Mavis, but the guilt of losing her babies has had a profound effect on her and has made her somewhat paranoid. Yet we cannot really be sure of what is true. Morrison leaves the question open. All we know is that Mavis had to escape, and this was not easy for her.

We get a clear and compelling portrait of Mavis. She is presented as undeniably negligent with her babies, but she may still be a good person and deserving of a second chance. On the run from an intolerable life, she finds and moves into the Convent, which will inevitably bring her into conflict with the people of Ruby.

She also meets two members of the Morgan family, one of the backbones of Ruby, as they had been in Haven. We get a definite impression of Soane, and although we do not learn much about her son (including his name), we may possibly learn it later. With this connection to the Convent and to Ruby, a storyline begins to take shape.

Here too there is mystery, particularly in the "you-know-what" that Soane Morgan went to get from Connie at the Convent. Soane makes sure the pouch is safe in the car, and Morrison makes a point

of not revealing what is in the pouch. Another tantalizing riddle comes at the very end of the chapter, when we read that Mavis is exhausted from the pleasures of the night before. Although we can speculate about the pleasure, the fact is that we can't really know exactly what kind of pleasure is meant.

Beyond this, the chapter has two possible themes in common with the first one. First, it describes a time of great difficulty, in which survival can be achieved only through drastic change. This time, a single woman's survival is at stake. Second, the chapter raises questions about the meaning of "paradise." After all, paradise is often thought of as a place. If the men in the first chapter are willing to kill to protect their town, maybe they feel that Ruby is their paradise. In this chapter, we see the world through Mavis' eyes. When she finds the Convent, she feels at peace, as can be seen toward the end of the chapter, where we read that the moonlit landscape Connie and Mavis saw from their windows was "Unjudgemental. Tidy. Ample. Forever." This suggests that the Convent is a paradise for Mavis.

Although the story told in this chapter is quite straightforward, Morrison's storytelling is subtle and full of hidden significance. This is especially true of the latter part of the chapter. We know that the Convent is an important place in the novel, and that every detail is there for a reason, from the moment when Mavis arrives at the Convent to the out-of-place odors that she smells at the very end of the chapter.

Study Questions

1. How did the neighbors react to the deaths of Mavis' twin babies?

2. What event surprised Mavis as much as it surprised everyone else?

3. How many times had Mavis been a patient at the County Hospital, and how many of those times were for childbirth?

4. What information from Mavis deeply disturbs her mother, Birdie Goodroe?

5. On what does Mavis get drunk when her car runs out of gas?

6. What are some of the unusual details about Connie?

7. What food does Connie offer Mavis? Does Mavis eat the food?

8. Why does Connie think that shelling pecans is a good job for Mavis?

9. What is the population of Ruby, according to the sign Mavis sees?

10. What did Mavis dream about the night after she first met Mother?

Answers

1. The neighbors seemed pleased when the babies died.

2. The event that surprised Mavis as much as it surprised everyone else was Mavis' stealing the Cadillac.

3. Mavis had been a patient at the County Hospital 15 times; 4 of them were for childbirth.

4. The information from Mavis that deeply disturbs Birdie Goodroe is Mavis' assertion that her family is trying to kill her.

5. When her car runs out of gas, Mavis get drunk on the Old Times whiskey her husband left in the car.

6. Some of the unusual details about Connie are: her hairstyle (described as Hiawatha braids), her fondness for aviator sunglasses, and her direct, almost brusque way of speaking.

7. Connie offers Mavis a potato, and Mavis, despite her nausea, eats and enjoys it.

8. Connie says that shelling pecans is a good job for Mavis, because Mavis has the perfect fingers and fingernails to do the job right and get the nut meat out whole.

9. According to the sign that Mavis sees, the population of Ruby is 360.

10. The night after she first met Mother, Mavis had a dream in which a lion cub attacks and eats her. The lion cub in this dream had blue eyes, just like Mother's eyes.

Suggested Essay Topics

1. What do you think of Mavis? Describe her based on what you learned in this chapter. Evaluate her strengths and weaknesses. Would you want to have her as a friend? Why or why not?

2. What are your impressions of the Convent and of the two women we meet there, Connie and Mother? What sense do you get of the place? Use specific details from the chapter.

Chapter Three: Grace

New Characters:

Gigi (Grace): *an outsider who comes to Ruby and goes to the Convent.*

K. D.: *the nephew of Deek and Steward Morgan, and the nephew described in the first chapter. As described there, he is spoiled.*

Good and **Ben:** *the two dogs K. D. tends at the beginning of the chapter.*

Arnette Fleetwood: *K. D.'s girlfriend. She is fifteen and pregnant.*

Billie Delia: *Arnette's friend. Billie has a reputation as a loose young woman. She, Arnette, and K. D. are among the group of young people who hang out at the Oven, a habit that the older residents of Ruby do not appreciate.*

Deacon (Deek) Morgan: *one of the leading men in Ruby. He and his twin brother, Steward, are the twin brothers in the first chapter.*

Steward Morgan: *the more outspoken of the two Morgan brothers. Steward has leased his ranch to a gas company.*

Arnold Fleetwood: *Arnette's father and one of the leading men in Ruby.*

Mabel Fleetwood: *Arnold's wife, a woman whose people played an important role in the histories of both Haven and Ruby.*

Jeff Fleetwood: *Arnold's son and Arnette's brother. Recently returned to Ruby from Vietnam, Jeff and his wife Sweetie live with his parents. He has a violent temper. He is ready to stand up for his family and very ready to fight.*

Sweetie Fleetwood: *Jeff's wife. Their children have been plagued by health problems. Some of the children have died; Jeff and Sweetie have four now. Mabel and Sweetie spend much of their time nursing them.*

Reverend Misner: *the town's main spiritual leader, who comes with Deacon, Steward, and K. D. Morgan to the Fleetwood house in order to help mend the troubles between the family. He is described as very handsome and possessing an impressive voice suitable to his calling.*

Mikey: *a boyfriend from Gigi's past; she seeks him in Arizona before giving up on him and winding up in Ruby.*

Dice: *the man on the train who tells Gigi about a strange landmark (two fig trees whose branches grow into each other) outside of Ruby.*

Roger Best: *the man who gives Gigi a ride to the Convent. His new van doubles as a hearse, and he uses it to pick up Mother's remains.*

Summary

A young man named K. D. is grooming a pair of dogs, whose ranch life makes their fur unkempt. As he does this task, he replays in his mind a recent scene and its consequences. A sexy young woman, a stranger, got off a bus in Ruby. Just by showing up she made waves, mostly by the way she dressed and walked: uninhibited, sensual, and provocative. She had an instant effect on the young men who were hanging around the Oven. They could hardly believe their eyes. The girls in the group were disgusted; one of them, Arnette, noticed the effect that the stranger had on her boyfriend, K. D.. She spoke her mind on the subject, and K. D. slapped her for what he felt was insolence. The slap quickly raised problems between his family, the Morgans, and Arnette's family, the Fleetwoods.

To rectify the situation, Reverend Misner arranges for K. D., Deacon, and Steward (K. D.'s twin uncles) to accompany him to the Fleetwood home; it is this meeting that preoccupies K. D. as he grooms the dogs. For although the fact has not been officially disclosed, Arnette is pregnant, and K. D. is not about to settle down with her. Arnette's decision, based partially on her desire to go to Langston in the fall (it is now August), will further tarnish the Convent's reputation.

None of the Morgan men are happy to visit the Fleetwoods, because their home is ruled by illness. The four very young children of Jeff and Sweetie (Jeff is Arnette's brother) were born barely alive, and have remained so ever since. Jeff, recently returned from Vietnam, radiates anger.

The meeting to hash out the offense is understandably tense, and the tension worsens dramatically when Steward makes an unkind reference to Arnette's upbringing. This brings Jeff into the fray, and the conflict seems about to escalate, but K. D. stands up and apologizes. The discussion continues.

The next morning, Reverend Misner considers the previous night. The rage that had filled the room had unsettled Misner, he likens it to a bear that was never truly tamed. Also, he remembers the reception he got from the two women of the house, Arnette's mother and sister-in-law. Mabel Fleetwood was receptive to his efforts to be charming, but Sweetie seemed distant and untrusting. Misner is unable to let go of the animosity he has witnessed. He considers the men involved and concludes that K. D. is a despicable young man.

The story then shifts to explain Gigi's origins. A man from her past, Mikey, is scheduled to get out of jail, and they have plans to meet in Wish, a town in Arizona, which has an unusual landmark: a rock formation that looks like a man and a woman making love. Unable to find either the town or the landmark, Gigi decides to go home to Mississippi and her grandfather.

During a train journey, Gigi meets a short man named Dice. Their first contact concerns Dice's disagreement with a snack-counter clerk, and Gigi speaks up for Dice. The two begin to talk. He tells her about a different landmark—a place where two trees grow into each other next to a pool of clear water. Intrigued, Gigi asks where it is; Dice replies that it's near Ruby, Oklahoma.

Gigi steps off the bus into Ruby. In her first two minutes in the town, she is vaguely aware that she has stirred up something between a boy and his girl. The boy is K. D., who soon follows Gigi to the Convent; their liaison will be the source of future problems. But Gigi doesn't take long to decide that there isn't much to see or do in Ruby and is ready to move on.

Trying to get a ride to the train station, Gigi is brought to the Convent by Roger Best, who is going there in his capacity as an Undertaker.

While waiting for Roger in the Convent, Gigi wanders around and finds, among uneaten food and general emptiness and neglect, a strange old woman asleep on the floor. It is Connie, who is exhausted and vulnerable after Mother's death, which was just the day before. Connie asks Gigi to stay with her while she sleeps, and Gigi stays, although in doing so she misses her ride to the train station. When Connie wakes, they talk briefly, and Connie asks Gigi for her real name, which is Grace.

Analysis

In many ways, this chapter is similar to the previous one. We read about two worlds: that of Ruby and that of the individual. Both worlds are enduring all manner of strife. Specifically, a woman makes her way, largely by accident, to Ruby and to the Convent. We find minor or barely existent characters, such as Mikey and Dice, who operate as foils for the main characters. It will not help the reader to get bogged down by focusing on figures in the story who are merely mentioned; *Paradise* is too big a work for that. Though we may get some kind of impression from Dice in the train and the quietly noble way in which he handles an unpleasant snack clerk, his role in the chapter is to get Gigi to Ruby.

From there she finds her way to the Convent, which feels, as it did for Mavis, like home to her. Also quite important is that, as in the previous chapter, the reader gets a chance to know Gigi on her own terms. Although it might be easy for some of the residents in Ruby to demonize her, we might feel that Gigi is simply a headstrong young woman trying to discover the world for herself. Keep in mind that the older citizens of Ruby think that being old-fashioned is a very good thing. This means that her new ways are bound

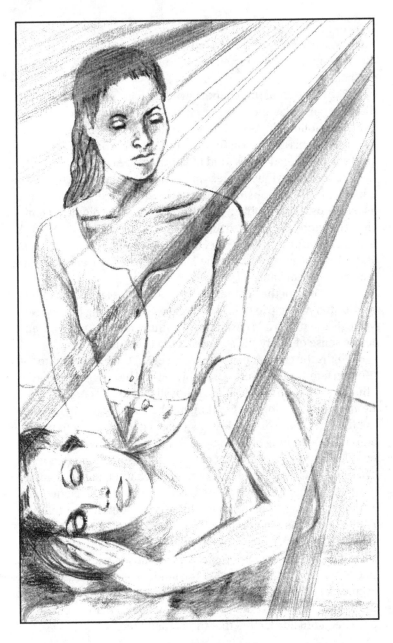

to cause difficulties. She never wishes to hurt or lie to anyone, and she is clearly able to form friendships; this would seem to make her a sympathetic character. But to the people of Ruby, she is unwelcome.

The first part of this chapter switches back and forth between the original incident (Gigi's arrival and K. D.'s slapping of Arnette) and what follows it. As K. D. tends to the dogs at the beginning of the chapter, his mind is on Gigi's arrival, which amazed him; it was as if she embodied a new kind of knowledge. Arnette's caustic response to his obvious interest motivated the slap, which in turn raises a fairly serious dispute between the Morgans and the Fleetwoods. Their problem involves pride and the dignity of families. Therefore, the insult to Arnette, and to all the Fleetwoods, has a symbolic aspect to it. The Fleetwoods are an important family in Ruby, but not as powerful as the Morgans, who own, among other things, the local bank.

At the end of the chapter we are back with Mavis, who comes home after a long trip to find the naked Gigi sunning herself. Mavis feels the powerful sensations of coming home, to Connie and to the sense of safety she so loves at the Convent.

This is the chapter in which we meet K. D., who belongs to the Morgan family. He is young, probably 18, and he has been told from childhood that he is special. He is not shown to be considerate. As he attends to the dogs, K. D.'s thoughts become a gateway, for they are the start of the history lessons we will need in order to understand the beginning of the novel. We learn that Steward and Deacon, K. D.'s uncles, are twins and the grandsons of a great man. This clues us in to a large part of the first chapter, and we can begin to put together some of the pieces of the puzzle. Notice that Morrison allowed herself quite a few pages before she told the reader about the men in the raid described in the first chapter.

We also get the feeling of the great weight of history. K. D. feels secure about the upcoming meeting, because he knows that the uncles will seek to protect what the family has worked so hard to accumulate. What is interesting is that now they have to protect their interests against their neighbors, whereas before there may have been outside factors that threatened them.

We might wonder why Jeff and Sweetie's babies are so frail. Is there something amiss in Sweetie's reproductive system? Or is there some other reason? Steward and Dovey, for example, are unable to have children. Jeff's tours in Vietnam may have exposed him to some horrible chemicals there. Perhaps there is a deeper, even more unpleasant reason for the birth defects. The perceptive reader will get a hint of something in a later chapter.

Study Questions

1. Whom does K. D. remember in connection to the lace he sees in the house?

2. To what does Deek liken the credit union Misner has founded?

3. What specific memory comes back to K. D. when he thinks about this new woman, whom he so desires?

4. What does Reverend Misner say that the Fleetwood women promised to bring out?

5. When Reverend Misner sees K. D. speeding down a street, what is the young man driving?

6. According to Dice, what, other than the fig trees, makes the town of Ruby worth visiting?

7. How had the citizens of Wish, Arizona, reacted to their local landmark?

8. How does Dice respond when Gigi tells him she hates rhubarb?

9. How much did Roger Best charge for the removal of Mother's body?

10. How much time had passed between Mother's death and Mavis's return to the Convent?

Answers

1. K. D. remembers his Aunt Soane in connection to the lace he sees in the house. He remembers that she worked lace like a prisoner, making more lace than could ever be used.

2. Deek likens the credit union Misner has founded to a piggy bank.

3. When K. D. thinks about this new woman, the memory that comes back to him is of a time when he was a boy. While traveling with his uncle Steward, K. D. once saw a big swimming pool, full of white children and outside his reach. He never forgot it.

4. Reverend Misner says that the Fleetwood women promised to bring out coffee and rice pudding after the men have their family meeting.

5. Reverend Misner sees K. D. speeding down a street driving Steward Morgan's Impala.

6. According to Dice, the other thing that makes Ruby worth visiting is the rhubarb pie a person can get there.

7. The citizens of Wish, Arizona, hated their local landmark and wanted to destroy it with explosives.

8. When Gigi tells Dice she hates rhubarb, he says that she "ain't lived at all."

9. Roger Best charged 25 dollars for the removal of Mother's body.

10. Seven days had passed between Mother's death and Mavis' return to the Convent.

Suggested Essay Topics

1. How would you describe the conflict between Gigi's way of living and that of the citizens of Ruby? Look at the information in this chapter and think about how Ruby is described in the first chapter. What similarities and differences do you see between the rules that govern this young woman and how this community of individuals lives? Could people learn from each other in this situation? What problems might develop?

2. What would you say are Gigi's best and worst qualities? We see her interact with many different people in this chapter. Do you think she is a good person? Why or why not? What words would you choose to describe her, and why?

Chapter Four: Seneca

New Characters:

Dovey Morgan (nee **Blackhorse**): *wife of Steward Morgan and sister of Soane Morgan. She worries about her husband and the future of her town.*

Menus Jury: *a man who lives in Ruby; a member of one of the founding families. He served in Vietnam and has a drinking problem.*

Reverend Pulliam: *one of Ruby's three spiritual leaders. The reverend of New Zion (Methodist) Church, he represents the old ways of thinking and decries the behavior of the youth of Ruby. His first name is Senior.*

Destry Beauchamp: *a young man who speaks up at the town meeting. He and his brother Royal challenge the old notions about the message on the Oven, and they are not very respectful to their elders.*

The Friend: *a mysterious but friendly man who visits Dovey Morgan on the porch of their little house in town (as opposed to their ranch outside of town). Neither Dovey nor the reader ever learn much about him.*

Elder Morgan: *the older brother of Steward and Deacon. He does not appear in the novel, but remains a figure in the memories of the twins. Although Elder had many children, they did not stay in Ruby and are not included in the novel.*

Rector Morgan (Big Daddy): *the father of Elder, Steward, Deacon, and (the late) Ruby Morgan. Like his father, Zechariah, Rector remains a figure in the memories of the twins and is featured in* the stories/history lessons told by the invisible narrator. He helped his father, Zechariah, along the dangerous journey to found the town of Haven.

Zechariah Morgan (Big Papa): *Rector Morgan's father and one of the founders of the town of Haven. He is a shadowy, almost mythical figure, because there are few clear memories of just what kind of man he was. Zechariah was an ironmonger, and he put the message on the Oven's door.*

Anna Flood: *the proprietor of Flood's General Store. The daughter of Ace Flood (one of the founding fathers of Ruby), Anna is very aware of how power and influence operate in Ruby. She is in love with Reverend Richard Misner.*

Seneca: *a young woman who is wandering aimlessly. Abandoned when she was five, Seneca is meek and very accommodating to others. She became involved with a young man in prison.*

Jean: *Seneca's sister, who abandoned Seneca.*

Eddie Turtle: *the young man with whom Seneca becomes involved. He is serving a six-month sentence in jail, and Seneca brings him a Bible. He is mean and abusive to her.*

Mrs. Turtle: *Eddie's mother, whom Seneca visits in Wichita, Kansas. She is not hospitable to Seneca.*

Norma Fox: *a mysterious woman who "hires" Seneca for some private services. She is young, well-dressed, and attractive, with champagne-colored hair and red-painted toenails. She picks up Seneca in a limousine, in Wichita.*

David: *Norma's chauffeur, who approaches Seneca about employment.*

Leon Fox: *Norma's husband. He does not appear in the novel.*

Summary

The chapter begins with Dovey, who is Steward's wife, remembering her wedding. Also getting married is Dovey's sister, Soane, who married Deacon; two sisters marrying twin brothers. As we learned in the first chapter, this double wedding took place in 1949; the present year is 1973. It seems that Dovey was happier then; life with Steward has not been easy. Dovey cannot help but think about her husband in terms of everything he's lost, from his land and hair to his sense of taste. There is one other thing lost that is deeply painful for Dovey; the couple has never had any children. And that was due to Steward.

Dovey, still brooding, thinks about Ruby, and the troubles her town has seen in recent times. She runs through a list of people: unruly teenagers, the town drunk, daughters who talk back to their mothers, people out of control. She knows that the meeting tonight will probably not help matters any.

There is a serious problem between the generations. As we saw in the first chapter, the Oven is central to Ruby's identity, and any discussions about it are bound to bring on strong emotions. That is the atmosphere at the town meeting, which is held in Reverend Misner's church. The meeting concerns a major debate over the Oven, specifically the words and message that the first Morgan had placed on the lip of the Oven's iron lid so many years before, in 1890.

Part of everyone's distress about the Oven centers on a form of graffiti put there by, it seems likely, one of the younger citizens of Ruby. It is an image of a black fist, and it has political implications. This is 1973; the upheavals of the 1960s, including Black Power and the deaths of Martin Luther King and Malcolm X, have already shaken the country. Only now, quite a few years later, are these events making themselves felt in Ruby. The elders of Ruby see the gesture as destructive, because any change to the Oven is unacceptable to them.

The change on the Oven is indicative of something larger, and there are other, more serious issues beneath the topic of the Oven. The youth of Ruby have their own view of the world, and of their place in it. They have clearly been influenced by Reverend Richard Misner, and their view of the past conflicts with that of their elders. Several young people, none of whom have any other role in the novel, speak stridently about their ideas and perceptions. They challenge their elders and show them little respect. The way the youth address their elders provokes hurt bewilderment from the older women and dangerous rage from the older men. The debate is settled by Steward, who threatens (indeed, promises) swift death to anyone who tampers with the Oven.

After the meeting, Dovey asks Steward to drop her off in town, where they have a little house; Dovey enjoys spending time there. Her sister Soane lives nearby, and Dovey loves to see the town's gardens. Her thoughts about the gardens allow the invisible narrator to give a brief history lesson. As time went on in Ruby, people could do more than just get by. More money came in, which introduced all kinds of home improvements and fancy appliances, which in turn changed life even more by increasing the amount of leisure time available. People turned to hobbies and to making their homes as beautiful as possible.

There were elements of pride in this wealth and leisure; competition became part of life as well, for suddenly people were trying to outdo one another with the size and splendors of their flower gardens. It became a divisive part of life. Yet Dovey, who loves to cultivate her garden, is still grateful for the beauty around her home.

But there is yet another reason to be there. A man comes by from time to time, a stranger with whom Dovey likes to converse. His visits are infrequent, and they never last long, and though the two of them never do anything more than talk pleasantly, Dovey remembers the details of their conversations and thinks of them as a private world that gives her great satisfaction.

Dovey has to search for the key to let herself into the house. This annoys her mightily, for she is certain that theirs is the only locked house in the town.

Meanwhile, driving away from town, Steward mulls over not only the meeting but also some of the issues he sees behind the problem. He feels that this younger generation (the one that spoke up so stridently at the meeting) has already lost much of the knowledge and understanding they will need in order to really make it in this world. His opinion of Misner is falling, and his sense of hope for Ruby's future is not bright.

Steward compares people today to those of the past, when expectations were demanding and clearly understood, and no one failed to do what was necessary. Perhaps he feels at least slightly uncertain about what course of action to take so as to help preserve the future (though it seems unlikely that he would ever admit this to anyone). Steward concentrates on the past, remembering stories that he has memorized; this is the connection between his thoughts and the narrator's opportunities to give history lessons.

One of these stories is about his brother, Elder Morgan, coming back from World War I in 1919. Elder saw a black prostitute assaulted by two white soldiers; before he knew what he was doing, he had intervened with violence and then, prudently, made for home with all speed. The story had stayed with Steward ever since he heard it.

Later, while riding his horse on his land, Steward is entirely preoccupied, brooding on a flood of memories and other impressions of the past. The reader learns about a very powerful story, coming from a mythical past. This story is about Steward's grandfather Zechariah and the exodus from Mississippi and Louisiana to, eventually, their as-yet unborn town of Haven. The people endured many kinds of hardships, but kept their spirits. At one point they needed and received help. One night, Zechariah took his son, Rector, into the woods, and Zechariah knelt and prayed. While Zechariah was praying, Rector was scared by the sound of giant footsteps. Zechariah and Rector suddenly saw a vision of a small man walking away from them. Whether it was God, an ancestor's ghost, or neither, is never explained. They followed it to their new home, where they built their Oven immediately. But through it all, they were angry and upset about the worst of their trials. The people were rejected by other black towns in the West. This was an extremely important event in their history; it defined their future.

The story then shifts to Soane, who sits in her kitchen, relaxing after having completed a few household tasks. Deacon ("Deek," as she and others call him) is out hunting quail. Soane knows that Deek's need to go out and hunt has to do with his anger and frustration over the meeting.

Many thoughts waft through Soane's mind, and most of them disturb her. She thinks about her dead sons—how she had felt, or at least hoped, that they would be safe. She thinks about the daughter she never had, who would have been 19 if she had been born.

Thoughts about this miscarriage bring a swelling of guilt and misery into Soane, who brews a special tea mix she got from the Convent (the mystery package she had picked up, along with the pecans, in the second chapter). Soane's thoughts shift from her own personal misery to a world that has been changing so quickly, and losing so much—this is especially noticeable in Ruby. She won-

ders how the town's ills might be healed and whether going back
to a simpler time, when things were so much better, is possible.

Deek comes in with his quail. The two talk about various subjects, including the Convent women and their dead sons. It is clear
that the couple has some issues that disturb them both.

Later in the morning, Deek feels some peace. He follows his
usual routine, yet his mind is on history again. The reader hears
about many things, including the death of Deacon and Steward's
sister, Ruby. This story is horrendous. She had been in decline for
some time, and eventually it was time to "give in" and take her to a
hospital. The nearest was in Demby. They went there, and then they
went to Middleton. Because of the Jim Crow laws in effect, they
could not find a doctor who would see Ruby in either hospital. Ruby
died on a waiting bench, and the brothers learned that the nurse
had been trying to contact a veterinarian. This was a humiliation
almost beyond all endurance. The brothers carried their dead sister in their arms back to their town (which at that point did not
truly have a name).

When they buried her, their powerful prayers, all their deep-
seated hate, anger, optimism, hope, and strength worked together,
to form a kind of strange magic. They may actually have made a
deal, a pact, with God. And since that time (it appears to have been
almost 20 years, from 1954 to 1973), no one has died inside the
town of Ruby. The other part of the arrangement is that there have
been practically no marriages, or children born, outside of their
select group of the founders and the children of the founders. The
repercussions of this "arrangement," which was all the more powerful and binding for the fact that no one ever actually admitted
that it existed, can be seen throughout the novel and contribute to
many of the town's problems.

The story shifts again to Anna Flood's general store, where she
and (Reverend) Richard Misner talk. She rails a bit about the
Deacon's habit of cruising around the Oven, as if he were a police-
man looking for criminals. Deacon has already decided to talk to
Anna and suggest that she keep that area tidy, because the young
people who hang out there buy their snacks and smokes from her
store.

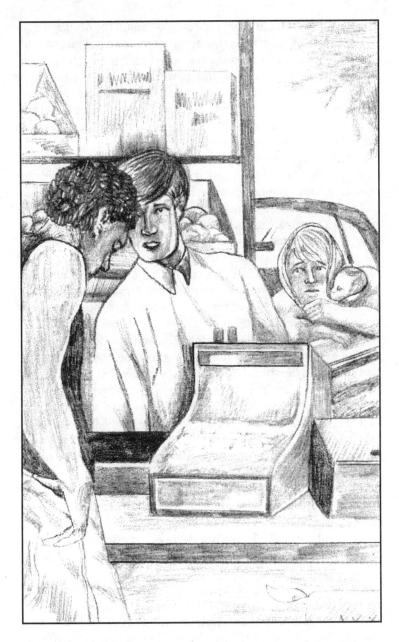

Richard Misner listens as she goes on about the Morgans and their arrogance. He asks her questions or makes comments about her perceptions of life in Ruby. In a way, she is teaching him about history; Anna explains how things work in Ruby (even though Misner has been in Ruby for three years). It is clear from their conversation that they disagree about who has, or should have, the power in town. Anna's resentment is countered by Richard's reasonable and peace-making tones of voice.

While they sit and talk, a stranger comes in. He is a white man in city clothes, and he is worried for several reasons. His wife in the car outside holds a sick baby, and they are on their way home to Texas. He asks about the town drugstore, which he cannot find because it is unmarked and looks just like a private house. Richard Misner immediately offers to go there and bring back medicine; the man buys some supplies from Anna.

The man is shown in a sympathetic light, but he does not listen to cautions about the bad weather that is on its way. After they leave, the sky changes—at first it turns beautiful, but then ominous snow begins to fall.

The story shifts to Sweetie, Jeff Fleetwood's wife. In this foreboding weather, she leaves the Fleetwood home. Steward Morgan had come into the store as the family of strangers left, and he mentioned that Deacon had seen Sweetie walking through town. This startled both Anna and Richard. Sweetie had not exactly planned to leave; her head is empty of thoughts. She seems fixated on the idea of escape, but she would never really let herself think this outright because of the guilt it would provoke. She has no plans and cannot truly notice the world around her.

The next part of the chapter cuts quickly back and forth. One story is the present. Sweetie is exhausted almost to madness now with caring for and worrying over (and probably feeling guilty about) her babies. She leaves the Fleetwood house without a plan of where to go. The weather is unwelcoming, and she wears only a thin housecoat. She is in some danger.

Finally, a young woman leaps off a truck to help her. She is Seneca, and once she joins the story, the narrative backs up and tells her life history. We meet a little girl who was five years old when she was abandoned by her "sister," Jean; the reader later learns that

Jean was a 14-year-old mother. Bounced around to foster homes and sexually assaulted, Seneca grew up very shy and unable to speak up for herself. She became involved with Eddie Turtle, who was in prison for six months for an unspecified offense. He treats her badly. For example, the only Bible she can find is very large, and he complains caustically about this and other things.

Eddie asks her to visit his mother, who lives in Wichita, Kansas. Seneca does so. Mrs. Turtle is unfriendly, serves only poorly cooked vegetables, and does not offer Seneca a bed for the night. Yet Seneca, a compassionate young woman, sees that Mrs. Turtle, despite her claims to not care about her son, is wracked with pain and grief.

While waiting for a bus to leave Wichita, Seneca is "offered work." Though the reader is never explicitly told what the work is, Seneca has clearly been propositioned for prostitution. A well-dressed chauffeur asks her to talk to his employer in a limousine. The woman in the stretch-car is Norma Keene Fox, a stylish and attractive woman, who appears to be in her late thirties. She talks with Seneca, who is slow to realize that the car is already moving. Seneca stays with Norma for three weeks; the two play different kinds of "games," some sadistic and some tender. When she leaves Norma's home, Seneca has the 500 dollars that she had been promised.

After that, Seneca begins to drift again. First she hitchhikes but then finds that stowing away in the backs of trucks is simpler. It is while doing this that she sees Sweetie. Seneca can tell instantly that something is wrong, and she wants to help. She joins Sweetie, who by this time has walked quite a long way from Ruby. They reach the Convent, where Sweetie is unable to appreciate or even recognize the kindness and solicitude of the women there. She feels that the women are crowding her and trying to seduce her into evil ways.

Sweetie leaves the next morning, finds her way into the arms of her husband, Jeff, and gratefully returns to the life she had left behind. For Seneca, a new life is beginning at the Convent.

Analysis

"Seneca" is the longest chapter in this novel and develops many subjects. Far more than in any of the previous chapters, it opens wide the world of Ruby.

During the meeting, we learn of the message on the Oven, which was alluded to in Chapter One. However, we don't really find out what the message is, because the first word is missing. Because so much time has passed, the citizens of Ruby themselves can't be sure what that word was. To them the message is, "the furrow of his Brow." Traditionally, the elders of Ruby have said that the first word was "Beware." The meeting is largely about how a new generation of Rubyites wants to interpret the message; they feel that the first word was, or should logically have been, "Be." The older Rubyites will not entertain other interpretations of something so sacred; their memories of the Old Fathers of Haven are a ruling force in their lives, and therefore any change equals death. They feel a need to defend themselves and their past from this newest threat, which comes, for the first time, from their very children.

The younger citizens act as though they need to be heard. It seems clear that Reverend Misner has been acting as their advocate, simply by encouraging them to seek connections between themselves and the rest of the world. Misner's political (and therefore, to some extent, his pedagogical) position will be more fully explained later; for the moment all we need to know is that he exhorts the youth to think about themselves and the world as parts of the same puzzle, instead of cutting themselves off from everything else.

Morrison has two techniques for making the reader's job difficult. The first technique is something we already know quite well: her tendency to drop hints about a character or a character's story and then withhold the rest of the information until many pages later. The other technique is something that was not used as much in the previous chapters: Morrison revels in an effortless ability to switch from a character's thoughts into a deep-level history lesson. Such lessons have come up in all of the chapters before this one. Here, history becomes more of a character itself, and Morrison spends more time on the past than she has done earlier. This habit will continue for most of the remainder of the novel.

As we shall see in a later chapter, Morrison names many, characters; the majority of them are never truly included in the interwoven stories that make up this novel. For example, there are over a dozen young people who hang around the Oven. Their habit infuriates the elder Rubyites, who still think of the Oven as too important to treat in this way—it should be reserved for special events and treated with respect always, not sat upon or vandalized.

As an example of the lengths that Morrison goes to in order to paint a full portrait of the town, there are over a dozen young people around the Oven, including nine boys from four families (two Sargeant, three Poole, two Seawright, two Beauchamp,) and four girls (two DuPres and, at least formerly, Arnette and Billie Delia).

None of these young people are given ages or even first names. Yet if the reader was to begin to keep a list of characters in Ruby and then draw lines to keep their relationships clear, that reader would start to understand the complicated webs of family trees in this town. Of course, not everyone has the kind of time and determination that this might require.

Is this information essential? Not really. Yet if we pay attention to how people are related, and try to keep family relationships in mind, we will have a better understanding about life in Ruby, and therefore a more full experience of the novel. Much more family information is still ahead.

Some of the chapters briefly describe people who are only to be left behind. Overall, many names are mentioned without a corresponding character coming forth. Of all the many Ruby citizens who are mentioned in this chapter, none of the new names are as important as that of Menus Jury, whose name comes up over a dozen times in the novel. He will take part in the raid on the Convent. Although he never speaks, or appears as a "real" character in the novel, Menus' story will tell us quite a bit about Ruby and about the interactions between the town and the Convent. For this reason, we should not forget him.

Similarly, the lost visitors, who are not townspeople and who occupy only two pages of this chapter, will also be important, and we should not forget them. Morrison used a brief moment of an ordinary day and showed how it could affect the future. The lost visitors and their fate will be mentioned several times in the coming chapters.

Dovey's conversations with the man she calls "the Friend" are important because they are so unusual. This is one of the few times that a stranger visits Ruby repeatedly. Gigi stays out of town, and others pass through, but the Friend is more mysterious. It may well be that this mystery, and its implied freedom from restrictions, are what causes Dovey to have such an interest in him, and what brings on the pleasurable nervousness she feels when he calls.

Dovey is somewhat worried that their conversations will be noticed by someone passing by. We might even wonder if her interest in him qualifies as a kind of infidelity, although not of the physical kind; she has opportunities to speak and act in ways that she cannot with Steward; she is not controlled by people's expectations of her. This explains why she tends to ramble when the Friend visits. Perhaps we might even consider that when the Friend visits, the clamp on her mouth has been removed.

The Friend could go on the list of the novel's mysteries, because no one in this small, very closely knit town claims him as a relative or friend. Although we do not get much of an impression of him, we learn enough to know that he is not the same person as Dice, in the previous chapter. Ultimately, the mystery of the Friend's identity is like that of whether or not Mavis was really in danger from her family—not important in the larger picture of the novel.

A discussion of one spouse may tend to be incomplete without commentary on the other. Another element of Dovey's story is Steward. As we learn about him in this chapter, we can see how he and his brother Deacon differ from one another.

It might be useful to recall the seemingly vague portrait of them that we read in the first chapter: "The brothers approaching the cellar were once identical. Although they are twins, their wives look more alike than they do. One is smooth, agile and smokes Te Amo cigars. The other is tougher, meaner, but hides his face when he prays."

Then, in the third chapter, we learned a crucial fact during the meeting between the Morgans and the Fleetwoods: "Steward, known for his inflammatory mouth, had been cautioned by Deek to keep his mouth shut and let him, the subtle one, do the talking."

Now, in "Seneca," we are getting a clearer idea of how the brothers differ. Consider the almost-hidden insight into Steward that accompanies his memory of Elder in Hoboken in 1919. Elder, just returned from World War I, sees men assaulting a black prostitute and leaps to her defense. Steward admires Elder for his courage, yet also feels a kind of connection to the white officers and imagines himself in their place, doing what they did to the woman.

In essence, he dreams about doing violence to this woman. Why would he feel this way? When speculating about a character's motivations and private psychology, any answer will be one reader's personal theory. To answer the question, it could quite possibly be because, as a prostitute, the woman brought shame to her color. By being weak and reducing herself to the position of a slave (not controlling, or even outright owning, her own body), the woman was bringing her people back down into the dust.

This is the first chapter to truly focus on the community of Ruby, and we have several indications that the town might be in trouble. Both the debate over the Oven's message and the way in which the debate ends tells us about how people in Ruby communicate.

By most standards, Ruby is like any other small Western town. Its citizens rely on hard work and have to endure trying weather conditions and the unpredictable factors that go with working the land. Their triumphs made them satisfied with their efforts and themselves—this too can be found throughout the West.

Most of all, Ruby, like many homogenous communities, does not wish to change, but wants instead to enshrine the past and remember its lessons forever. This is impossible, especially as the pace of events in U.S. history in the second half of the twentieth century was picking up speed. Most of the country is embroiled in the Civil Rights struggle, an important era, but the elders of Ruby could not be bothered with such things. They have their own idea of freedom, and as far as they're concerned, they've been living that idea for as long as they can remember. For the youth of Ruby, though, it's a different story.

At this point in the novel, we know quite a few of the basic facts. The Convent is blamed for, and finally attacked because of the pressures on the townspeople. The reader might begin to suspect that the townspeople's concerns may not have their true source in the Convent.

This raises many questions: Why did the town begin to falter? Why do they lash out at the Convent? The answers are connected, of course, and to answer them we would have to list every single part of the novel, from the eternal contentiousness of human youth to the temporal changes of politics in America.

Might the community of Ruby be doomed? Maybe it's too early to tell. What is the solution to its problems? It does not seem that anyone who lives there is able to do anything about it. They all try, but the characters, especially the Morgan brothers, are stuck with what they know. They have no answers and cannot see beyond their limited situations. Invisible forces, many of them internal, threaten the town.

The crux of their problems is the clash of the past with the present. The elder generations, who had direct experience of extreme hardship and had to struggle for every benefit and amenity, developed iron wills and were strong leaders. Even those who followed the founders, who grew up more comfortably, heard tales and learned from their elders and were imbued with the spirit of their heroes.

But something happened, or perhaps a combination of factors. The thread of continuity has been lost, and the young, who grew up surrounded by ease and plenty, did not understand why strictness was necessary.

The present does not live up to the past, and the elders see what once was successful is now fading and failing. An example of this is the disappointed hopes of the Morgans. They, who had thrived for so long, are now at a dead end. Elder Morgan had many children, but his family scattered, leaving Ruby far behind; therefore, his family line could not be counted on.

Deacon and Soane had two boys, both of whom died in Vietnam, and a girl, who was either stillborn or died very early. Her death is linked to something that happened in the Convent. Steward and Dovey had a series of miscarriages. K. D., the son of their sister, Ruby, was the sole heir to the bloodline, which is the only proof of survival. And he is a disappointment all on his own.

But the history is always there; by learning the story of the past, we see why it carries such a weight in the present. Zechariah's people have had a very long history in this country. They lived and traded in Louisiana before the United States of America even existed. They held important positions and had good reason to be proud of their accomplishments. That pride grew larger as it was passed down, for once the old ones were gone, their faults and shortcomings could be conveniently forgotten, and they would end up enshrined as holy in the minds of their descendants.

At the same time, however, the humiliations borne by the Old Fathers of Haven remain fresh and painful memories for the New Fathers of Ruby, who, unlike their predecessors, never had to ask for any aid on the way to their future home.

We learn that there are three churches in this town of 360 people: the New Zion (Methodist), the Calvary Church (Baptist), and the Congregational Church. The fact that a town of this size has three churches might indicate that religion and spirituality play a central role in the town. As we can see in this chapter, however, the churches only contribute to the fragmentation of life in Ruby. Witness how the other churches laughed to see Misner's flock divided, as the youth that he had possibly "riled up" caused considerable consternation to their church community. Soon the effects of this were felt in the other congregations, as well. Overall, the reader would do well to consider how religious and mythological themes operate in this novel.

Although Christianity is the only religion officially recognized in Ruby, it is not the only element of religion or spirituality in the novel. Throughout the novel are hidden small indications that other forces hold sway over the characters' perceptions of reality, both at the Convent and, even, in the town. By and large, these have to do with nature and dreams, both of which are noticed and taken seriously by one or more characters.

When Anna Flood remembers how her return to Ruby from Detroit provoked a lot of reaction in the town, because she came back with unstraightened hair, the reader is shown something about how Rubyites see themselves and perhaps wish to be seen by others. Most of the older town folk disapproved, in a variety of ways, of Anna's hairstyle, whereas the younger citizens were not merely accepting, but even, some of them, highly approving.

It seems clear that the question of hair, and whether or not to alter it, is important in the novel, as it has been important in African-American social history. For women in particular, the decision to straighten or not to straighten their hair stirs a complex mix of feelings about race, identity, pride, culture, and beauty. During the 1960s and 1970s, not straightening one's hair was a highly politicized act, and was part of the "Black is Beautiful" movement. Anna's choice, which came from a place outside of town, provided the

town's youth with an example of other ways of viewing and inter-
acting with the world. Do not forget the social upheaval for which
the 1960s are famous; this is a moment from those times. Like many
other threats to the feelings of old-fashioned security cherished
by Ruby elders, this idea came from the outside world, which earlier generations had not explored very much.

Study Questions

1. During the debate about the Oven, to what had Deacon
   Morgan taken exception?

2. How did Dovey Morgan feel about the issues in the debate?

3. What kind of food had Dovey offered the Friend when he
   visited?

4. What had Soane shouted when she saw her sons at Thanksgiving in 1968?

5. How many quail had Deek killed while hunting?

6. How many towns did the Morgan men and boys plan to visit?
   Did they get to all of them?

7. Why did Deek decide not to go after Sweetie?

8. How did the hitchhiker manage to avoid injury when she
   leapt out of the truck?

9. How did the Convent women seem to Sweetie when she arrived?

10. What was Seneca considering doing when she was ap-
    proached by Norma Fox's chauffeur?

Answers

1. Deacon Morgan took definite exception to someone referring to his grandfather Zechariah as "a former slave."

2. Dovey Morgan felt ambivalent and undecided about the issues in the debate.

3. Dovey had once offered the Friend a slice of bread and apple
   butter when he visited.

4. When she saw her sons at Thanksgiving in 1968, Soane shouted, "Prayer works!"

5. Deek killed 12 quail while hunting, 6 of which he had given to Sargeant Person.

6. The Morgan men and boys planned to visit seven towns, but they visited only four of them.

7. Deek decided not to go after Sweetie because he felt opening the Morgan bank on time was a greater responsibility.

8. The hitchhiker (Seneca) avoided injury because the truck was climbing an incline.

9. The Convent women seemed like predatory birds to Sweetie.

10. When she was approached by Norma Fox's chauffeur, Seneca had been waiting for a bus and was thinking about going to see a movie.

Suggested Essay Topics

1. What do you think of Seneca? What impressions do you get from her? Review the chapter carefully and combine the facts given with what you feel and might assume about her as a character. Support what you say with details.

2. What is your impression of Ruby, based on what you have learned in this chapter? How do you see its problems, and what solutions might you suggest, if you had the opportunity?

Chapter Five: Divine

New Characters:

Pallas Truelove: *a young woman with a troubled past. She appears to be a child from an interracial marriage. Originally from Los Angeles, she runs away from home and eventually finds the Convent.*

Carlos: *Pallas' boyfriend. He was the janitor at the exclusive girls'*
   school she attended. He is much older than Pallas. He eventu-
   ally leaves her for her mother.

Summary

The chapter begins with K. D. and Arnette's wedding ceremony.
It is three years since her pregnancy and the incident between their
families, as described in "Grace." The event is the setting of a battle
between the two main spiritual leaders of Ruby: Reverend Pulliam
and Reverend Misner.

The chapter opens with Reverend Pulliam addressing the
room; he is a guest preacher in Misner's Baptist church. Pulliam's
words are harsh as he tells the bride and groom, and everyone else
attending, that love is not the weak, easy thing they all seem to
think it is. Love might be God's gift to mankind, but love that is not
on God's terms is nothing but delusion and stupidity. God, and
God's rules, will always come first, and couples who marry without being in accordance with these rules are doomed.

Not very surprisingly, this is uncomfortable to hear at a wedding, and everyone is embarrassed and somewhat ashamed, which
may be what Pulliam wants. But it seems clear that he is carrying
forth in this manner for the benefit (or, in this case, for the hin-
drance) of someone not involved in the wedding itself. Many people
in the church are sure that Pulliam's words are designed to trouble
and hurt Reverend Richard Misner, whose ideas of God and God's
love, and the social implications of these beliefs, are very far from
what Pulliam himself believes.

In fact, Pulliam's speech has hurt Misner so badly that Reverend Misner cannot even trust his own ability to respond in a self-
controlled manner in that crowded room. For now, after Pulliam
has held the floor for a time, it is Misner's turn, although the congregation is already looking forward to the reception and all the food
and fellowship they hope will accompany it. The whole town thinks
of this wedding day as a day of healing, for there have been far too
many times of ill will between the Morgans and the Fleetwoods over
the last three years. Although no one is sure what happened to the
baby she was carrying, everyone assumes that she went to the Convent and that they "took care of it." This abomination has not been
forgotten.

Now Misner, unsure about how to master his anger at Pulliam, and at himself, decides to forego the sermon he had prepared. Instead, he goes to the back of the church and takes up a large cross. Holding it cradled in his arms, he steps before the congregation and is silent. He hopes to show them a mystery, an image of a silent black man that will move their hearts. He wants to put on a symbolic display for them, to be eloquent without speaking. Most of the audience there feels very frustrated in their desires that the ceremony will continue and be done with so that they can move on with their lives.

K. D. is angry; he feels that every moment is a kind of petty torture, that far too much attention and pressure has been focused on him for too long already. He replays the past three years, ever since he and Arnette have been involved; it is a time full of details, many of them unpleasant. He simply wants the future to carry him, and them, forward into better stories.

Even more than her husband-to-be, Arnette is desperate to have the ceremony over with. The last three years have been considerably more painful for her than for him. She wants to be accepted as a real woman and wife. At the moment, that acceptance feels jeopardized. All of the good feelings that planning the marriage raised are dashed to the ground by the clock agonizingly ticking the seconds away.

Billie Delia, like K. D., is impatient, but for different reasons. She is looking forward to starting her life outside of Ruby, because she has had enough of the abuse that life in the town has been for her. The narrator launches into Billie's story and the moment that her life began to change.

Billie was three years old and loved to ride a particular horse, the same horse that won the first race in Ruby, which K. D. had ridden to victory. When Nathan DuPres had ridden Hard Goods down a street, offering rides, Billie Delia took off her fancy panties there in the street so as to better enjoy the ride. She didn't know that this would be considered inappropriate—the response to that small incident changed her life, for the worse. Now, though still a virgin, Billie Delia has a reputation as a loose young woman, and she has had enough of life in Ruby.

Steward Morgan is surprisingly patient, but then he is not pay-ing much attention to the service. He remembers a story about his father, Big Daddy. He was coming back to Haven with important medicine for the town when he got lost after sunset. In the dark-ness he could see a campfire, and then on his other side he heard music, laughter, and gunshots. He could go in either direction, toward what could be either shelter or death. Big Daddy finally decided to head for the campfire and was welcomed by the men there. He then learned that the town was dangerous, with a sign that said "No Niggers" at one end of the town and a cross at the other end. Steward thought to himself that "a cross was no better than its bearer."

After an interminable silence, with Misner holding the cross, the ceremony itself begins. Soane almost has to restrain Deek, who is angry now. Soane herself is in turmoil and cries at the wedding for two reasons: because of the sad yet hopeful smiles of the bridal couple (who had already been through so much trouble), and at her own apprehension and guilt about the fact that she, in poor judgment, had invited Connie (and, therefore, she feared, the Con-vent women) to the reception. She worries about the confronta-tion between the women and some of the townspeople.

Soane had a dream that indicated an ill omen, in which her dead sons chide her for leaving fancy chicken feathers in the kitchen sink. She interprets the dream to mean that the coming conflict between the town and the women is like a storm and will cause damage.

At the reception, the tensions between the townspeople are dissipating. There are smiles and music, despite the less-than-en-tirely pleasant wedding ceremony. But just when people begin to breathe more easily, the blast of a car's horn is heard. The Convent women have arrived. As could be expected, they are not consid-ered welcome visitors, and their visit does not go well.

The women are on their way home from Ruby. The narrator describes the feelings of each of the four women, without naming any of them. The women seethe with the feelings that their inter-action with the Rubyite men have raised. It does not take much for a confrontation between Mavis and Gigi, who have never gotten along, to bloom into a real fight.

The car pulls off to the side of the road as the pair spills out, punching, kicking, and hairpulling with determination. The other two passengers, Seneca and Pallas, hold each other for comfort. A truck comes up the road; the driver, who had planned to stop and help, sees the women and changes his mind.

The story now shifts to introduce Pallas. We find out that, unlike the other women at the Convent, Pallas came from a well-to-do background in Los Angeles. Yet she too has been wounded by various moments and elements of her life. Pallas has a recurring memory of something she had seen in a fancy shopping mall in Los Angeles: a crazy woman who for some reason deeply upset Pallas. But beyond this, Pallas is reeling from the turmoil of an ill-chosen liaison. Her poor relationship with her father has made her vulnerable and needy, and she became involved with Carlos, her school's janitor. They made plans and drove off together, from California to her mother's home in New Mexico, where Carlos and Dee Dee, Pallas' mother, became lovers. After that, Pallas wandered aimlessly, until she ended up at a medical clinic, where Billie Cato (whom we know as Billie Delia) found her and took her to the Convent, a place where Billie herself had once gone for a short time for refuge.

Pallas is slow to settle in and feel comfortable. She is even slow to speak. But a brief conversation with Connie helps, as does the sensation of eating. Even Gigi's unpleasantness and insults do not keep Pallas from staying, partially because she has nowhere else to go.

The reader is given insights into the other women who have come to the Convent. Seneca is cutting herself; she has a whole set of rules and rituals about her self-mutilation. The narrator supplies the story of how Seneca started doing this. Gigi, meanwhile, has found a hidden metal box and feels certain that it contains great amounts of money or gold or jewels.

But the most arresting of these stories is that of Mavis. The feeling Mavis had when she first came into the Convent, that her children were there, is growing ever stronger. The spirits that she perceives comfort her. And better still, the ghosts/angels/spirits of her twins love their spirit-sibling (the ghost of Arnette's baby), and they also love Pallas.

At the end of the chapter, a brand-new bride appears at the Convent threshold. She is Arnette, who has come to ask for her baby by K. D., three years before. However, it seems that the baby has died. Although we are not shown what follows, it appears that when Arnette is told about her baby's death, a vicious fight begins. For Mavis and Gigi, it is the second fight that day. We can only imagine what happened when Arnette returned to Ruby, crying (as she probably was), in her ripped wedding dress.

Analysis

By the end of this chapter, the novel is past the halfway mark, and we have heard some of the stories that the narrator had summarized in the first chapter. The family with the four damaged infants is the Fleetwoods. Arnette is both the daughter who would not get out of bed and the bride who disappeared on her honeymoon (the brief mention of her staying in bed comes from the first pages of the fourth chapter, "Seneca"). Some of the stories from the first chapter have been explained, and others remain to be told. Some new stories have begun since that first chapter, and they have yet to explained. The reader can be confident that many of the open-ended stories will be resolved by the novel's end.

One of the newer mysteries is the tale of Menus. We learn in this chapter that he was at the Convent; on their way home from the reception, Gigi complained about all the cleaning up she had to do when he was there. Why was he vomiting and defecating all over the place? Then we remember Menus' drinking problem: He went there to get cured. This revelation helps the reader get a sense of the women's compassion.

As stated earlier, Ruby is like many other Western towns. The great majority of the American West has always been, and still is, sparsely populated. The biggest difference between large cities and small towns is that whereas there is a sense of anonymity in the former, just the opposite is true of the latter. In a small town, everyone knows everyone else, not only by name, but in a personal way, somewhat like an extended family. In the same way as in a family, there is a sense that each person is, at least to some extent, accountable to everyone else.

The only way that a group of people who share a common bond, such as a religious conviction or an ethnicity, can maintain an identity different from that of the outside world is if every member of the group continues to be faithful to the traditions laid down before them. When people begin to stray from what is considered appropriate behavior, the community is in serious danger of unraveling. People must not question their group's ways of being. If they do question, then they must be controlled and brought back into the fold.

Inevitably, people will wander from the path of "correct" thoughts and actions; this is especially true given the passage of time. We have seen examples of Rubyites who have more or less broken the town's unwritten rules, including the youths who spoke at the meeting. Even Anna Flood, by changing her hairstyle, caused trouble.

In this, as in almost every other chapter, we see the older generation's attempts to control the younger Rubyites. Most of the examples are subtle; if they were brutally obvious, they wouldn't work so well. There is a moment at the reception when Alice Pulliam goes to Anna Flood and Kate Golightly (another almost mysterious Rubyite, for she never appears in a scene on her own and is only barely identified in a family) and asks them what they think of the Convent women. Alice Pulliam's remark about brassieres is designed to warn Anna and Kate away from such disgusting displays as indulged in by the Convent women.

Another example of control is the case of Menus Jury. Having missed their chance to keep Roger Best on the straight and narrow, the men of Ruby were quick and determined not to make the same mistake when Menus fell in love with "the pretty sandy-haired girl from Virginia." Menus lost his house in town (the foreclosure that Dovey and Steward moved into, which we read about in the previous chapter) and began to drink.

It is this need for control, and the rigid thinking behind it, that greatly frustrates Richard Misner. What especially angers him is the way "over and over with the least provocation, [the people of Ruby] pulled from their stock of stories tales about the old folks, their grands and great-aunts; their fathers and mothers." This over-reliance on and idealization of the past at the expense of the townspeople's own lives is a theme that Morrison will explore in later chapters.

Interestingly, the character whom the reader might have expected to be a major presence in this chapter is elusive and difficult to know. That is Pallas, the newest addition to the Convent. Unlike the last three chapters, this one does not bear the name of the woman herself; Divine is, as we learn, Pallas's mother. More importantly, we might have noticed that throughout the previous three chapters, the new "main character" has, each time, less and less of a presence. In other words, Mavis clearly dominated her chapter; the "camera" of the narrator's gaze was focused on her, and there was little to no information about Ruby or the people there. Even when Rubyites came into the story, they were described as little as possible.

In "Grace" this changed somewhat. Though we got an impression of who Gigi was, she interacted with the town from the chapter's very first paragraphs, and we were shown the people of Ruby to a far greater extent than before.

In "Seneca," this trend continued. The long chapter contained relatively little about Seneca and much more about the history of Ruby and its people, including the distant past. Seneca herself was relegated to the end section, and we were rushed through her life history, quite unlike the treatment we saw for Mavis.

Now, in "Divine," very little of the chapter is devoted to the new character. We are given very little idea of what Pallas looks like (but then, Morrison says almost nothing in terms of physical description for any of the characters). Not only this, but we get no sense at all of her personality, beyond two facts. The first fact is that she fell for an older man, one who quite possibly did not grow up in affluent surroundings, as she had done. The second fact is that she felt deeply hurt and victimized when she found her lover and her mother together. This is her trauma, and it seems to define who she is.

Some book reviewers have commented that several of the novel's characters, especially the Convent women, were woefully underdeveloped and merely two-dimensional, robbing the novel of narrative power. Other reviewers, however, have found Pallas and the other women to be compelling despite their lack of specific development.

Study Questions:

1. What name did Anna Flood use when she thought about Reverend Pulliam?

2. Which biblical verses had Misner planned to allude to at the wedding?

3. What animal-related incident were various people interpreting as an omen about the wedding?

4. How did the groom respond to this supposed "omen"?

5. What had K. D. done with the letters he received from Arnette?

6. What biblical verse had Reverend Pulliam featured in a sermon about Arnette's "outrage at the Convent"?

7. What were some of the manifestations of the trouble between the Morgans and the Fleetwoods?

8. Who begins to play the piano at the wedding reception?

9. What did Billie [Delia] Cato specifically warn Pallas not to be worried about at the Convent?

10. What kind of job does Gigi assume Pallas' mother held?

Answers

1. When she thought about Reverend Pulliam, Anna Flood used the name "Senior 'Take No Prisoners' Pulliam."

2. Misner had planned to allude to Revelation 19:7 and 9, and Matthew 19:6 at the wedding.

3. Various people at the wedding were concerned about the buzzards (vultures) seen flying north over the town. They interpreted this as a bad omen about the wedding.

4. The groom's response to this supposed omen was one of scorn. He felt that those who paid attention to it were simpletons.

5. K. D. had put the letters he received from Arnette in a shoe box in his aunt's attic.

6. The biblical verse Reverend Pulliam featured in a sermon was Jeremiah 1:5.

7. Some of the indicators of the trouble between the Morgans and the Fleetwoods included the time Jeff Fleetwood pulled a gun on K. D.; the time Menus Jury had to stop a shoving match between Steward and Arnold Fleetwood; and the time Mabel Fleetwood didn't send a cake to the All-Church Bake Sale.

8. Kate Golightly begins to play the piano at the wedding reception.

9. Billie [Delia] Cato specifically warns Pallas not to be worried if she sees the women in the Convent walking around naked.

10. Gigi assumes Pallas' mother had been a stripper.

Suggested Essay Topics

1. Why would religious differences in Ruby add to the difficulties the town is having? How might the people who founded Haven, so long before, have avoided these problems?

2. One character we learn far more about in this chapter is Richard Misner. What had we learned about him in the previous chapters, and what new information and insights does this chapter provide? How has your opinion of him changed?

Chapter Six: Patricia

New Characters:

Patricia Best: *mother of Billie Delia and daughter of Roger and Delia Best; she is a schoolteacher.*

Nathan DuPres: *the oldest man in town. He tells a story from his childhood at the Christmas production. (He tells the same story every year.) He is also the owner of Hard Goods, the horse that K. D. Morgan, when he was a small boy, once rode to victory in the race at the founding of Ruby.*

Summary

Patricia Best is at home, but she is thinking about the upcoming Christmas play. She is certain that it will be the same as every year before. She is a little tired; she has been listening to her father, Roger Best, rhapsodize about his grand business schemes. But her mind is full of thoughts, some of them troubling, and she decides to go upstairs and work on her "project."

Unbeknownst to the people of Ruby, Pat Best, the schoolteacher, is also the town's unofficial historian. As such, she is trying to compose the town's history. One might expect that the people of Ruby, who in general, seem distinctly proud, would hardly mind sharing their families stories, but Pat finds that people are very reluctant to tell her much. They do not appreciate her efforts to dig into their pasts.

Pat's collection of family trees expands as she pieces together an assortment of information, including stories told over the years, gossip and rumors, and anecdotes gleaned from her students' personal essays. As her project progresses, Pat realizes that the notations are less and less fact-based and more intuitive and subjective. The work becomes a private hobby, as Pat goes into great detail about the lives of her neighbors and their families.

As part of her speculations, Pat considers the reasons why people and families have grown the way they did. She thinks first about K. D. and Arnette's baby, which is expected soon, according to Lone DuPres. The narrator tells the story of Lone, found and rescued by the original settlers of Haven. Arnette's first baby is a mystery, except that everyone assumes that they know what happened, that Arnette got an abortion at the Convent. But now, Arnette, safely married, is expecting another child.

Pat believes, at least at first, that the Morgan brothers are highly interested in their nephew's wedding because K. D. is the sole remaining heir to the Morgan money. Then another thought occurs to Pat. She has placed the symbol "8-R" next to the names of the founding families of Ruby. This symbol comes from the vocabulary of coal mining, and signifies "8-Rock," the darkest coal that comes from the layers deepest in the earth. She uses the symbol to stand for the skin tone of the members of these families.

Pat has long known that the leading families of Ruby share one important attribute-all of them have remarkably dark skin, as blue-black as the coal that comes from deep in the ground. Obviously, a physical trait such as this is inherited—it's genetically based. What Pat comes to realize is that skin tone is profoundly important to the social history of Ruby. Pat can tell that this preoccupation with skin color has affected many people's lives. It is common knowledge that, over the years, there have been marriages within families. Such things did not happen often, but it was understood that, when a spouse died, or when a young woman "did not have prospects," an older relative would "take her over." Pat's own husband, now long dead, was the child of such a marriage.

The revelation about the 8-Rocks has a great effect on Pat. It both scares and fascinates her, but most of all it disgusts her. She has always been keenly aware that her family was never accepted in Ruby, and she knows why. The main reason is that Roger Best, her father, was the first man to break the unwritten laws that safeguarded the racial purity of Ruby's founding fathers. He married Delia, a white woman. Menus Jury also wanted to marry outside of his color but was dissuaded from doing so.

Pat mentally addresses her dead mother as she writes and tells her mother a story of her own death. Through the writing, Pat tries to explain that many of Ruby's women tried to help but were stymied by their men, who refused to assist. Pat explains just what happened, and why the people of Ruby behaved the way they did.

Pat continues to examine her family's poor standing in Ruby. In addition to his marriage, her father is looked down upon because he is the town's undertaker. Although it is generally a necessary job, undertaking has never been a very popular trade because it is associated with profiting from others' deaths. This is even more true in a town like Ruby. The first body that Roger prepared was that of his wife.

Pat thinks about the fact that no one has died while they were in Ruby. People from the town who have died did so elsewhere—while traveling, overseas in war, or at the hospital in Demby. That no one has actually died in the town itself has, she feels, given the citizens a prideful notion that death cannot touch them as long as they stay in Ruby. She wonders if eternal life might just be the deal that the Morgan brothers seem to have worked out with God; pure 8-Rock blood equals immortality in Ruby. "Marry" your own, she thinks, and you will never die.

Another family member looked down upon in Ruby is Pat's daughter, Billie Delia. Pat now thinks deeply about Billie Delia and their relationship. She thinks in particular about two memories and how they might be connected. The first memory is the story of the day when little Billie Delia, only three years old, pulled down her panties to have a horseback ride. Pat knows that her daughter was mistreated because of that incident, but Pat is also honest enough with herself to recognize that she herself was part of that mistreatment.

The second memory is the more recent and traumatic and concerns the horrendous fight between them. The fight escalated immediately; the iron in Pat's hand slammed into the wall next to Billie's head, and Billie pushed her mother down the stairs. Fleeing the house, Billie caught a ride out to the Convent. Their relationship has not been the same since then.

The narrative now shifts, abruptly, to the school's Christmas show. Just as Pat had predicted, Nathan DuPres speaks, telling a story from his childhood. Pat observes the action on the stage and the audience. Richard Misner approaches her, and the two have a tense conversation, which is actually more of a debate. It moves from Billie Delia to relations in the town in general. The two differ about the importance of their collective past—of Africa. They clash over the best way to educate the youth of Ruby. As he sees it, they have been kept ignorant of their collective past. The talk turns more personal as Misner denigrates Pat's view of the world. Understandably, her feelings are hurt. In the meantime, Richard plays through various concerns, including his interest in moving on, to a parish where he might be treated better. The two trade a few more barbs.

During this time, the Christmas play is going on, and the audience responds very intensely. The scene plays out the town's history and the "Disallowing" endured by the founders of Haven.

Reverend Misner is troubled by their talk, but afterward he gains some peace of mind. He realizes that efforts to keep the youth in ignorance is Ruby's weakness; yet, it also means that this is a place where he can really help the youth get in touch with the outside world. His efforts to do this are not appreciated by the more established citizens of Ruby, who do not have any interest in what has been taking place in the rest of the country.

After the Christmas play, ideas about Ruby's hidden agenda are more and more on Pat's mind. She feels that her whole life has been affected by these efforts to control her. She realizes that she holds the proof of their efforts. At the end of the chapter, Pat burns the papers, yet she seems to have misgivings about having done so.

Analysis

Unlike the subjects of the previous chapters, Patricia Best has lived in Ruby her whole life. She is an observer with a definite point of view. In the comments she writes in her history project, and in her conversations with Richard Misner, we see her probing and somewhat judgmental mind. Pat's notations provide the reader not only with more information but also with a new voice in the novel. Hers is a distinctive voice, one that is critical and incisive, with a hurt, vulnerable quality.

Another female voice of commentary and criticism is that of Anna Flood. Though she spends her time in this chapter debating, internally, whether or not to marry Richard Misner, we should note why she vacillates. It's not a question of whether or not she loves him, but whether or not she has the endurance to be his wife and continue to watch the way he is treated. We also get a window into the "competition" between Anna and Pat. Richard is not only a handsome man, but he is an outsider, free of the biases the women have grown to hate.

Also important to note is that whereas Pat and Anna represent critical female voices, no men from Ruby are critical of their town, at least not in the same way. The Morgan twins, and possibly other men, envision a return to "the old ways," but do not question the status quo. Only Richard himself, an outsider, wishes to see a change. Even after the last several chapters, in which we learned so much about Ruby, there is still more to learn.

As we have seen, everything in *Paradise* is there for a reason and serves a purpose. The Christmas production is important for several reasons. The story of the play combines the story of the birth of Jesus with the tale of the founding of Haven. The story was never written down and took place over 80 years before. Only a few people in Ruby were there, for very few people alive in 1890 would be alive in December 1974, when the chapter is set. But everyone who watches the play knows the story.

There are two facts that show us how important the play is to its audience. The first is that the play remains unchanged from year to year. This tells us that it fulfills the role of a ritual and helps people to remember it. The other fact is the audience's reaction to the play. Their emotions are obvious; it is as if watching the play both hurts and heals them. Yet there is another view as well: The re-creation of the same play every year could be viewed as a wallowing in righteous indignation. By linking their history with that of Jesus, Rubyites make it less and less easy for them to check themselves and question their attitudes. Perhaps the play is part of their problem. This is especially true when we consider that although "the story of the play combines the story of the birth of Jesus with the tale of the founding of Haven," there is nothing in the play that connects it with the Nativity itself. Although the narrator does comment "the little lord Jesus lay down his sweet head," this is not in reference to the play, which never mentions the baby Jesus. Morrison calls the scene a Christmas play and then reveals that the pageant is really about the descendents of Ruby. This gives the play a somewhat blasphemous quality and further contributes to the theme of how the citizens of Ruby idealize (and idolize) their past.

Reading this part of the chapter shows us how storytelling has a central role in the community of Ruby, just as we have seen it at work in the novel. Although every chapter contains a good deal of history, especially from the third chapter onward, this chapter is the most history-based, especially because we see a historian at work, in the person of Pat Best.

But we are not yet done with the Christmas play, for there is at least one other message at work. Although the story of the play involves the town's past, it also involves the town's future. The people onstage are children—Ruby's future. These children are not the same group mentioned in "Seneca," the ones hanging out disrespectfully around the Oven. These kids are too young to have picked up such bad habits. Given what we learned in "Seneca," when Steward was worried about the town's future, some elders in

Ruby might think that everything rested on these people. Their exact ages are less important.

In the interest of showing what hard work Morrison put into building the town, and the hard work that the reader is invited to put in, these are the children: There are four Cary girls (presumably the grandchildren of Reverend Cary): Hope, Chaste, Lovely, and Pure. There are Dina and Joe-Thomas Poole (grandchildren of Aaron Poole), Linda DuPres (Pious's daughter), James Person (son of Drew and Harriet and probably the grandson of Sargeant Person), Lorcas Sands (son of Payne Sands), Steven and Michael Seawright (grandsons of Timothy Seawright), Ansel and "Fruit" Jury (grandsons of Peace and Solarine Jury and probably nephews of Menus Jury), and, probably much older than the rest of the children, Royal and Destry Beauchamp, both of whom are 16 years old. We have seen them before, in "Seneca."

Why the lists of founding families (the Old Fathers of Haven and the New Fathers of Ruby) are not the same, or exactly why some of those families are not represented on stage during the Christmas play, is almost explained at various points in this and other chapters. It has to do, at least partially, with the exodus from the Deep South to Oklahoma. The "nine large, intact families" picked up other people along the way; some were families or distant relatives of the original population, and others were lost children or survivors of disasters. Yet others were simply interested in the adventure. Despite the fact that these new people were part of the new town of Haven, Oklahoma, they were never truly included in the group of the founders. Presumably, this is because they were not "8-Rocks" and, therefore, not the right color. This must be tied to the fact that the number of families represented in the pageant has changed over the years. The citizens of Ruby chose not to celebrate the achievements, or even the presence, of those who do not share "8-Rock" blood.

In the middle of the Christmas play section of the chapter, there is a direct first-person address. The words are spoken in response to both the action on the stage and the audience's response to the play and to the specific scene they are watching. The speaker feels healed by the whole picture of actors acting out the collective history. The fact that this history is interpreted through a Christmas

tale involving the baby Jesus makes it that much more powerful. The speaker is warmed by the community's ability to use this little play, which is done the same way every year, to try to soothe and heal itself.

The words come out of nowhere, but one thing is certain: it is not quoted text spoken by a character. It is another mystery, yet it is different from the ones we have seen. The others had to do with content—that is, some part of the story, some action or attitude on the part of the character would be left unexplained until later. This case, however, is a matter of narrative. We have a speaking voice that is unidentified. Who is it that feels healed?

Two possibilities might occur to us. The first is that Pat, who observes the world around throughout this chapter, is addressing the reader directly. But this sentiment seems out of character for her, considering her distrust of so much of what goes on in Ruby. When we learn that Pat was disgusted by the audience's reaction to the play, we find that she cannot be the speaker of these words.

What is the other possibility? That Morrison's invisible narrator makes herself, himself, itself, visible. That either Morrison herself, the author, or the voice that records the intertwining lives of the communities in this novel, is speaking, saying that seeing the play is a healing experience.

As we have just seen, this chapter provides a flood of information about the families who founded Ruby. After sharing so little with the reader, Morrison lets loose a great deal of background. This part of the chapter is almost reminiscent of the book of Genesis in the Bible, with its pages of "begats." Once again, the attentive reader is constructing the town by imagining the people in it.

The genealogical information in the chapter is helpful, both in terms of the richness of life in Ruby and the themes that Morrison is trying to get across. It's almost as if the reader, who cannot contribute his or her physical labor to building the town, must instead work to put together the story of how the town came to be, where it's going, and why. One way of doing this is to figure out the relationships between the characters.

Once we succeed in doing this, we can see that some of the characters have been pushing the envelope of incest. Although Pat never explains the connection as simply as she could have done, we can see that Fawn Blackhorse (Pat's late husband's mother) had children with a man who had the same genetic makeup as her grandfather. The fact that he asked for and received permission to marry her and bear children with her makes absolutely no difference.

These kinds of practices are not talked about much in the town, and they may have something to do with why people are so uninterested in how their ancestors came to be married. As Pat notices, there are many women in particular whose family backgrounds are never known or explained; this might not be accidental, but rather a way of keeping secrets. Could those women whose families are never named be, in fact, from the same families as the men they married? This is an unsettling thought, but Pat's explanation of Billie Cato's family shows us how serious the people of Haven and Ruby are about their bloodlines. The more we think about this, the more we might wonder about Jeff and Sweetie's children, and why they might be so very unhealthy. Morrison never tells us exactly why they are the way they are. It could be for a variety of reasons, but one of those possible reasons is inbreeding.

Obviously, the "blood rules" operating in Haven and Ruby were, and still are, much more relaxed than those generally practiced in our society. Of course, there are many precedents for this kind of behavior in isolated towns throughout this country, even up to the present day. There is considerable documentation on the history of such practices. Inbreeding can happen in any isolated town, where the people are unable or unwilling to travel (or feel much safer in the town where they grew up, a town in which no one dies) in order to find a mate.

Perhaps Ruby's case is more like the histories of certain royal families in European history, who intermarried in order to maintain control of money and power. As far as Ruby residents are concerned, the men of Ruby have a kind of wealth they wish to maintain. It is their skin, that most desirable heirloom and remembrance passed on to them by their great and noble forefathers.

The fact that so many generations managed to maintain their especially dark shade of black is remarkable, given their long-term residence in what was originally a foreign country. Such a circumstance does not come about accidentally, or indeed without effort and sacrifice. But the preservation of skin tone, though it was never officially ratified, was equated with survival for the citizens of Haven and Ruby. It determined how people would know and accept each other, and, consequently, it became an object of control.

The people of Ruby think of their lives as individuals, and more in terms of community. For many, if not all of them, this is their conception of identity. They have learned from the lessons of the past and from all of the invisible instructions they picked up from their elders, which have shaped their biases and actions. Those lessons had to do with other people responding negatively toward them on the basis of their skin color. Their response has been to work, pridefully, to maintain that skin color.

It is quite possible that the reader, if he or she has never seen the grammatical usage "8-Rock" before, might find it confusing. We are never told whether or not there is coal in the area, or just why Pat Best would know the term "8-Rock." We can speculate that because Pat is a teacher, she would happen to know something about coal mining.

It is not a personal reference on Patricia's part and does have meaning outside of her private notes. There is a clue, hidden in the novel, that Pat did not make up the term "8-Rock" on her own, because the words have been introduced to the reader earlier in the novel. In the fourth chapter, "Seneca," there is a description of the goods sold in Anna Flood's store. One of the items sold there is "the black-as-eight-rock peppers from the Convent." A very careful reader might have caught the usage earlier, despite the way that Morrison tries to hide it by spelling out the "eight" instead of using the numerical sign, as it is used in this chapter. The phrase was placed there, more than 70 pages earlier, deliberately.

There is another kind of symbolism at work here as well. The peppers, which are mentioned at least once per chapter, were specifically cultivated, whether for their heat or their color. Peppers like these are the result of careful management; they were specifically grown to be this way.

In the same way, the people of Ruby have, to some extent, cultivated themselves for a specific color. This may seem a strange and disturbing observation, but we should not avoid asking questions about what Morrison is saying about race and skin color. Pride, including pride in one's race, can be a wonderful thing. But it is not always a wonderful thing, and is not, in itself, a virtue. The very black peppers appear too many times in the novel to be a casual subject. In fact the casual reference to the peppers in "Seneca," clearly links them with the Morgans, the Fleetwoods, the Blackhorses, the Catos, the Pooles, and all the other founding families of both Haven and Ruby. The connection between the peppers and the Rubyites is an important part of what Morrison seeks to illuminate.

There is another side effect of living with these 8-Rocks. Because it was men who decided to preserve their skin color, they needed to control the women who would give them babies and allow their ideal society to continue. This means that the women of Ruby tend to have fewer choices in life than they would otherwise have. The reader has seen this already. In the previous chapter, "Divine," we read about Billie Delia, who feels that her life was changed by what she saw and learned at the Convent. As some Rubyites might see it, the women at the Convent took part of their future away. The fact that Billie Delia might be thought of as not entirely desirable— for several reasons—is beside the point.

Ultimately, Ruby falls from paradise when its people start treating each other the way that they themselves were treated by outsiders in the past. From the first moment that the preservation of a specific skin tone became important, as a legacy of gratitude to the founding fathers, unwritten policies of racial purity began to govern all the citizens of Ruby. It was these policies, instituted by certain men and imposed with special importance upon the women (in a thousand subtle ways), that, possibly more than any other factor, did such damage to the community.

One major bombshell in this chapter is what Steward said about Pat's mother, Delia. Here we see absolute and hatefully cruel arrogance. It tells us that Steward has a lot of hate in his heart. It also sets the stage for Fairy DuPres' curse. Although a rational person might wish to think that Dovey's miscarriages (we never find out how many there were, or whether there might be another explanation for them) had nothing to do with what Steward said about Delia Best and were not the enactment of Fairy DuPres' curse, it is in keeping with the themes of the novel to sense a direct connection between what Steward said and his and Dovey's misfortune. The world of this novel does not lend itself to coincidence.

The ability to utter magic words (which is what Fairy's utterance might be viewed as) can be found throughout world mythology, as is the notion that midwives, as the people in charge of births, have special powers denied to other people. There is a brief discussion of this later in the novel. In fact the very idea that one person can "curse" another, and affect the future, is not something that one often sees in a realistic novel. But Morrison has used the technique before. This appreciation of mythology, which inevitably speaks to something deep inside all of us, is something that Toni Morrison shares with other African-American novelists writing today, including Alice Walker, Zora Neale Hurston, and Gloria Naylor.

As a final note (in keeping with the theme of history in this chapter and throughout the novel), this is a good time to consider the names of the characters. This chapter underlines exactly how important names are, because they are one of the basic ways by which we identify people and the way by which people show relationships between each other.

Names tell us almost everything. Just as Pat herself had commented on the possibility that "Missy Rivers" may have been named after, and therefore born near, the Mississippi River, and just as Deacon and Steward have names that suggest that their jobs in life have to do with watching over something, we can detect other stories within names. For example, Zechariah's born name was Coffee, and there are conflicting interpretations about this. Pat indicates that "Coffee" may have been a misreading of the name "Kofi," which was and still is a popular name in some African nations.

On the other hand, Coffee may have meant the drink, as in, "do you like your coffee black?" and might well therefore have been a reference to his skin color. One name has to do with his original identity as the descendent of an African, and the other may well have been a name given or associated with a past as a slave (after all, we know that the man who chose the name Zechariah for himself had been a slave); therefore, a desire to forget the slave name and take a new name, such as Zechariah, would be understandable.

Similarly, we find out that "K. D." is the character's nickname, not his real name. It stands for "Kentucky Derby," a reference to the horserace that he won as a little boy, at the founding of Ruby. This is an opportunity to apply American history to this novel, for as it happens, there is a long and illustrious history of African-American jockeys throughout the eastern states in the second half of the Nineteenth Century. The very first Kentucky Derby, in 1875, was won by a black jockey. This fact is not very surprising, considering that 13 of the 14 jockeys in that race were black. K. D.'s first name is Coffee, which was his great-grandfather Zechariah's original name. As also happens in real life, babies born in Ruby are very frequently named for their ancestors.

These kinds of details are important to a full appreciation of the novel.

Study Questions

1. What mistake had Pat made the previous school year regarding her students' Christmas decorations?

2. Were the Morgan brothers inclined to approve Roger Best's bank loan?

3. What did Pat look at in the yard through the open window?

4. What had Fairy DuPres fed the baby that she and her people rescued on the way to found Haven?

5. According to Pat's history project, how long had this particular group of "8-Rocks" been in this country?

6. What was left when Billy Cato died?

7. What exactly had Fairy DuPres said to Steward Morgan in response to his words about Roger's decision to bring and marry Delia?

8. How long did Billie Delia stay at the Convent?

9. How and when did Nathan DuPres and his wife, Mirth, lose their babies?

10. According to Pat's realization, is God's "Furrowed Brow" the one referred to in the Oven's inscription?

Answers

1. The mistake Pat made the previous school year regarding her students' Christmas decorations was to let her very young pupils apply the glue and glitter themselves. She had to clean their faces and hands.

2. Yes, the Morgan brothers were inclined to approve Roger Best's bank loan.

3. Pat looked at her mother's grave in the yard through the open window.

4. Fairy DuPres had fed the baby a water-soaked meal cake.

5. According to Pat's history project, the group of "8-Rocks" had been in this country since at least 1770.

6. Nothing was left when Billy Cato died except a few "effects," including a crushed gold ring.

7. Fairy DuPres had said, "God don't love ugly ways. Watch out He don't deny you what you love too," in response to Steward Morgan's words about Delia.

8. Billie Delia stayed at the Convent for two weeks and a day.

9. Nathan DuPres and Mirth lost their babies in a tornado in 1922.

10. According to Pat, the "Furrowed Brow" does not refer to God. It is the brow of Zechariah and those who followed him, of ancestors watching over their children and grandchildren, exhorting them to remain true to their (skin-based) identity.

Suggested Essay Topics

1. Why do you think Patricia reacted the way she did to her discoveries about the 8-Rocks? Do you think she did the right thing by burning the papers? Why or why not? What would you have done?

2. One of the many characters we have learned about is Billie Delia. Have your feelings about her changed during the course of the novel? Why or why not? What information do you feel is most important when it comes to understanding her? Who would you say is responsible for her troubles?

Chapter Seven: Consolata

New Characters:

Sister Roberta: *one of the nuns at the Native American girls' school.*

Penny and **Clarissa:** *two Native American girls (the last two, it seems, in the Convent's tradition of "educating" Native American girls), who look up to Connie and appeal to her for help.*

Lone DuPres: *Ruby's midwife and one of the town's oldest women. She helps Connie to explore and develop her abilities and, therefore, helps to bring Consolata out into the open.*

Piedade: *a mythical figure in Consolata's stories and lessons. Though described as a woman, Piedade has various powers and may be something of a shape-shifter.*

Summary

As Gigi said many pages earlier, Connie spends almost all her time in the cellar now. She does as little as possible, hardly moving from her dark, cool cellar, where she consumes bottle after bottle of the wine stored there many years before, by the sisters of the former convent. She has become broken in spirit and merely longs for death. The women and girls around her cause no feelings of sympathy but only rage and feeble hatred.

Connie was nine years old when she was rescued from a dead-end childhood by the nun who later became the Mother Superior at the Catholic school outside of Ruby. For 30 years Connie lived and grew up there, and the faith that she built fell apart the moment she saw a tall man in Ruby, when she was there on an errand with Mother. It was a forbidden love.

From almost the very first moment they saw each other, a personal energy was born between them, and though they each had obligations that should have precluded an affair, neither denied themselves the pleasure and connection that seemed so natural, and therefore perfect. Almost instantly, the two recognized something deep and powerful in each other, even beyond language itself. They escaped from the world together every chance they could.

Deek and Connie are very much in love, but their relationship is doomed. Steward approaches Connie, and Deacon feels the pressure of his brother's involvement; it's like a reminder of another set of priorities, the "rules" by which the town of Ruby was founded. Soane also talks with Connie, with serious consequences; Soane is pregnant but has a miscarriage. This was the baby she lost and was mourning, as she waits for Deacon to come back from his quail hunt.

In another place or time, Connie and Deacon might well have gotten married and raised a family. But that is not possible here, and the fact that Deek is married has nothing to do with it. He feels the pressures of the rules under which Ruby was founded. A life with Connie would break those rules, and this is one of the reasons why the relationship was doomed. Another was a moment when Connie drank Deacon's blood, an act that disturbed him. But all of that is in the past. Now, in the present, Connie has been in a great and determined decline.

Consolata receives an unexplained visitor in the Convent's garden. The visitor seems to be a man, but he is neither Deacon nor Steward Morgan, nor any other man from Ruby. This visitor is not identified by name, but his tea-colored hair and green eyes will allow us to place him later.

There is also Piedade, who is either a woman or a goddess whom others see as a magical woman. Although the lore of Piedade is an important part of the spiritual teachings at the Convent, the reader never hears full stories, with a beginning, middle, and end. It seems clear that Piedade is held up as a goddess, or perhaps simply as an ideal, but the stories about this mythical teacher/friend are important mostly through the effects they have on the women. Piedade has the power to move and change people, through song and through her very presence.

Through their visitations, Connie undergoes a transformation. She manages to rescue herself and then to rescue the small community of the Convent. She begins to cook good food and serves only water to those who live with her. She becomes what she was meant to be all along—their teacher. She takes charge of life at the Convent, telling the women there that life will be different and that those who are not interested in learning should leave.

Consolata soon has strategies for changing life for the women around her. One of these methods is to have them create "templates," a kind of floor painting with which the women can tell the stories of their wounds and troubles. This technique works well for them; it puts their pain outside of them, where they can see it. Life at the Convent is transformed; a new and wonderful sense of fellowship, love, and happiness is shared.

The last third of the chapter is made up of vignettes about the women who live at the Convent or are connected to it in some way—first Soane, then Pallas, Gigi, Seneca, and last, Mavis. As we read their encapsulated stories, we are brought back to earlier chapters, when we were first introduced to them. The biggest surprise is Pallas, who, after having left the Convent for a time, has come back pregnant and now has a son, a real baby in the Convent. But for each of the women, the world is recast as a place where they can really thrive. Another story touched upon is that of Arnette, who had come to the Convent for an abortion and then grievously injured her unborn baby by hurting herself.

For the reader, other pieces of who the women are now fall into place. They dance, and their dancing is the exhausting joy mentioned in the first chapter. The festering wounds of their lives are healed and resolved.

Analysis

This is a chapter of transformation. None of the present-day action is set in Ruby: there are flashbacks that explain the past, but the chapter is centered on the Convent and concerns how Connie, a broken figure at the chapter's start, regains her center and thereby effects a dramatic change in her community.

But who is Connie, and who is Consolata? Are they the same person, or not? In general, yes, but not exactly the same. It is likely that the little girl who was "kidnapped" was called Consolata. We were introduced to Connie in the second chapter. But the Consolata in this chapter acts differently than Connie did. It is important to take this difference seriously.

One clear aspect is that Consolata is the person who wakes up from the attempts to sleep and forget through drinking. Consolata is the one who rescues the women. In any of the references to the past, to other parts of her life, she will be "Connie." It is also the name by which the townspeople will always know her.

Morrison repeatedly reminds us of a few important things. One of those things is that the Convent is where the women who live there belong. They identify themselves with it, and although they do not have the long-term history with it that the residents of Ruby have with their town, the Convent is just as important to the women as Ruby is to the Morgan twins, Steward and Deacon.

Morrison's technique of telling us more of the story of characters we have already met is very effective. At the end of the chapter, we see that the women have made a kind of utopia and are different from the way they were when they first arrived. We feel more sympathy for them as we realize the extent of their troubles and their endurance as they strive for a better life. And we can feel joy for them as we see them finally coming together as a true community and having the life they have been missing.

It does not take long for the reader to figure out that "the living man" with whom Connie has a stormy affair is none other than Deacon Morgan. Morrison's prose is evocative as she describes the reawakening inside of Connie—this is a major turning point in her life. The same is true of Deacon; from the moment he sees her he is changed. That is why he does not need to really talk with her; until there are problems between them, language is unnecessary.

In retrospect, it makes sense that Connie has an affair with Deacon instead of his brother: There is a gentleness about Deek that Steward lacks. In fact, it is difficult to imagine Steward having enough passion to manage even having an affair! The man has lost so much, including his land and his sense of taste. The difference between them comes across twice in this chapter, as it has, in a variety of little ways, elsewhere in the novel; it will also be echoed toward the novel's end.

The first time is when the lovers are alone, by the two trees that grow into one another (which, we will recall, Gigi had heard about in the third chapter). Deacon reveals that he has a twin. When Connie asks about this, Deacon replies that there is only one of him. This indicates the distance that he feels exists between himself and Steward, as contrasted with what Steward had once said to Anna Flood, which was that for him, having a twin felt like a kind of security, even superiority.

The fact that Steward may have known about Connie's affair with Deacon is interesting, but not really one of the novel's mystical aspects. Many novels and films have explored the peculiar communications that twins have, and so Steward's manner while giving Connie a ride has something of a context. Besides, as Deacon himself suggests, it's possible that Steward was merely helping Connie out of what might have been a tight spot—a walk in Ruby does not seem to be quite as secure an experience for a Convent woman as for one of the town's women. Then again, Steward might just feel friendly, though that seems unlikely. Ultimately, the reader never finds out what Steward's reasoning was. Yet Connie has no doubts about their interaction.

The biggest and perhaps most unsettling mystery about Connie and Deacon's relationship is the turning point at which Connie bites Deacon's lip and enjoys lapping his blood. Deacon does not appreciate this kind of behavior and says so promptly. Connie's gesture seems out of character for her, but then we might have a hard time understanding just how much this relationship has allowed Connie to acknowledge and express her needs.

Which is not exactly to say that Connie needed Deacon's blood. Why then did she do what she did and act the way she acted? The answer is a combination of things most of which have to do with how she grew up. Connie was rescued from the street and brought up in a repressive environment, isolated at the Convent without many basic wants.

Connie does not complain about having grown up among nuns. On the contrary, she has been grateful for her life. Yet the reader can see that Connie has been missing a lot of life; she seems aware of this. The fact that she was rescued from poverty and sexual assault is wonderful, but not a guarantee of happiness. She has lived in exile, with very little freedom, especially emotional freedom. Small wonder, then, that Penny and Clarissa regard her as a role model, because they are also exiles, taken away from what was their home.

Most of all, Connie grew up without people who understood who she really was. She has no link to her home. Yet Connie identified with something in Ruby that day of the race. Did she love the town in general from the first moment she saw it? Not exactly. She identified with the mood she saw in the people, the way they moved and laughed with each other. The reader should keep in mind that on the day she had seen it, Ruby was at its most uncharacteristically playful; she saw the famous horse race, hardly a typical day for the community. The celebration in the streets set the scene for what immediately followed. Connie saw the man, and her entire world changed.

She sees something in Deek that makes her think of home; this has never happened to her before. In fact, she sees herself and feels far more complete when he is with her. What exactly does she see in Deacon? Morrison declines to explain, but it probably isn't (and certainly does not need to be) all that different from the deep, mysterious attraction that many couples experience when they are in truly in love.

Most of all, she saw something familiar in him, and she felt more whole in his company. It is obvious that she truly loved and trusted Deacon and would never have wished to harm him, physically or in any other way. Having been raised as a Catholic, she sought a kind of communion, in the literal sense of joining. We can speculate about whether Connie would have liked him to consume her, just as she seemed to want to consume him.

Whether or not this is true, it is clear that her act came out of an emotional need and not some perverse urging that involved deviant behavior or motives. Connie had the courage to seize the opportunity to pursue her own happiness, instead of remaining shackled by the obligations placed on her by others, and now, feeling secure in this relationship (more secure, apparently, than she should have felt; she moved forward with complete faith instead of doubting her partner), she gives full reign to her needs.

Although each of them has much to lose by pursuing their liaison, Deacon never commits himself as much as Connie does. Deacon is married and a prominent citizen of Ruby, but far beyond that, he cannot simply forget the almost-hidden injunctions that govern his conduct. It's as if, just as he and his brother supposedly made a deal with God, they made promises to the ghosts of ancestors, to those who came before. If he tries to ignore this pact, he will have to pay a great price.

As far as Connie is concerned, she has nothing less than her immortal soul to lose, and the love and trust of those whom she

had known almost all her life, who had saved her from a horrible childhood and raised her. Yet she feels that she has no choice but to follow the commands of her heart, which, as far as she is concerned, seems to be the same as her soul.

Connie and Deacon have one important thing in common: They are both hampered by, yet have the courage to break free from, the obligations put on them by others. Yet their courage is not equal, and they do not proceed in the same fashion. Connie commits her whole being, but Deacon never does. This makes him the more uneasy participant in their relationship, which he finally ends. But their affair will have repercussions throughout the rest of their lives.

Although Connie's feelings of isolation explain much of her relationship with Deacon, they do little to explain her mysticism. In this chapter we see two main examples of that mysticism—her ability to manipulate other people's life forces, and her stories about and visitations from nonhuman presences.

As part of her life story, we learn about Connie's conception of spirituality and God. Some of this is explained, but some is left to the reader to figure out. For example, the male pronouns "he" and "him" are sometimes capitalized, as is the standard practice in Christianity when referring to either Jesus or God. This we can attribute to Connie's upbringing in a convent, but Consolata's "god" may not be the same as the one that the nuns recognize. Connie's life story is fairly straightforward, but there is a great deal of background information to piece together in order to appreciate the story of her inner life. This information will help explain both her powers and the beings who visit her.

For example, where exactly is Consolata from? There is mention of Puerto Limon. A quick perusal of a world atlas reveals two towns named Puerto Limon in the South American country of Colombia, which is a good starting place for our understanding of the character. Even if we did not know this, however, and were not interested in applying real-world research to this novel (though it is only logical to do so, considering that this novel is, more than anything else, a historical tale), there are several clues in this chapter that suggest that Consolata is South American.

First, we learn that Connie, as a little girl, was picked off the streets by nuns serving an "Indian and Colored Peoples" order.

Then we are told about the girl's brown skin and sense of wonder at all the modern conveniences. Lastly, the fact that the ship makes a stop in Panama on its way to New Orleans means that it must have come from South America. Logic is enough of a basis to confirm this suspicion; it would also explain, for example, Connie's feelings about the dancing in Ruby.

Ultimately, the reader need not be very surprised at Consolata's religious conflict or about the kind of spirituality she ends up with. Once we consider her place of birth, we can speculate on the different traditions at work inside her. Whereas Catholic churches may be rare in Oklahoma, they are quite common throughout South America, as are various other religions, including, for example, voodoo.

In fact, one of the reasons that ritual is so important to Voodoo (and its many geographically specific types: Macumba, Candomble, and Santeria, to name a few) is that the teachings of the Catholic faith, which is also ritual-heavy, lent themselves to assimilation into the faiths already there. These Voodoo-related faiths have often been perceived as anti-Christian, and it is not surprising that people from Ruby, if they were to see the templates on the floor and the candles, would assume that they were seeing evil acts.

Rubyites are empiricists; that is, they rely solely on what they can see and hear. Although their relationship to God is still important to them, their church life has degenerated from something that rocked their everyday world into little more than a social convention and includes a good deal of political emphasis. The Convent women are quite different from this—for them, participation in their religion is more subjective; also, they have to worry far less about judgment from their neighbors.

The different ethic, or relationship to spirituality, is confirmed when Consolata is described as being "fully housed by" the god that visited her in the garden. This is a common occurrence in various Voodoo-related ceremonies, and, although it seems akin to the tales of "possession by spirits," it is not necessarily evil.

In Ruby, people are fully in control of their religious sentiments—the same is not true for Consolata. She participates in her own mythology.

This is a lot for the average reader to handle; clearly, Morrison is throwing a lot of things together. She wants to show the complexity of human life, and doing this will inevitably involve spirituality.

Readers may also wonder about the practice of "stepping in" and manipulating a person's inner light. Such practices are definitely outside the general realm of experience, and most of us will not be able to identify with Consolata's abilities. Once again, keeping a few things in mind will help us find a context for what she does.

First, we've seen that Connie comes from a different world than the other characters. Also, she is in singular circumstances—she has not had exposure to the outside world. She has led a secluded, sheltered life, protected from, yet also denied, the experiences most of us take for granted. She never had to strive for anything, yet she is not privileged, at least in the usual sense. All of these details would lead Connie to develop many inner resources, which she herself might not know exist.

We never get the impression that these "abilities" are the figments of the character's imagination; there is concrete proof of her abilities. Easter Morgan's life is saved, and Mother's life is prolonged by what Connie does. There is a recurrent observation that as she made use of her gift, Connie's eyesight deteriorated, as if staring into this other light ruined her eyes' ability to deal with everyday sunlight.

But in the final analysis, none of this matters. The reader is at liberty to interpret and judge Morrison's storytelling. The novel is historically based; by and large, the Rubyite characters act and make mistakes just as humans have always done—this makes *Paradise* quite realistic. Yet at the Convent, different rules apply.

There is a term, "magical realism," used to describe many novels and other works of literature written, most notably, by South American authors. It refers to the use of details and thematic elements that are magical and do not occur in real life, yet are included as if part of a realistic narrative. Morrison writes in this genre in *Paradise*.

The reader might become confused when Soane comes to the Convent, implying that she wants an abortion. We are shown no reason why she would want this. We have seen that the people of Ruby need to be fruitful and multiply. This is especially true of the Morgan family. The twins want to have big families but do not succeed in this.

We are never told why Soane didn't want the baby. The only reason that comes to mind is that she is worried that the baby will show that she has had an affair, but there has not been any indication that Soane had an affair with anyone (and there will not be any such indication).

This mystery has a solution. Careful reading of the crucial pages shows us that Soane was indeed pregnant but did not want to get rid of the baby. She used this premise as an excuse to go and see Connie, to "check out the competition," so to speak. Soane thinks of this urge on her own part as weak. The fact that she pretended, even if only for a moment, to want an abortion, was what, in her mind, brought about the spontaneous miscarriage. She played with fire by even speaking the words "I can't have this baby," and she was punished for it.

Soane attributes the loss of her baby to the punishment for arrogance. We have seen indications of arrogance before, such as Anna Flood's conversation with Richard Misner (in the fourth chapter) about Deacon Morgan's habit of patrolling the Oven. Anna feels that the Morgan family is arrogant. And Soane herself acted in a frigid and unfriendly way to Mavis, when the two first met. But perhaps the arrogance that Soane was thinking about was something larger than simply individual personalities, whether her own or anyone else's. Perhaps the loss of the baby is a larger punishment and judgment. This would be in keeping with the superstition and the involvement of mythology. Other things happen in the novel that do not seem to be coincidences.

We have noticed that Mavis seemed wonderfully adjusted to life in the Convent from the moment she first got there. More than for any of the other women at the Convent, it soothes and completes Mavis.

She has grown happier than when she first arrived. Her only problem is Gigi, whom she dislikes. But Mavis' life has inside it some darkness held over from before she fled her family. As part of her healing process, we have seen that Mavis has created an elaborate fantasy about her children, Merle and Pearl, who died at the beginning of Chapter Two. Although they died through her neglect, she loved them. After all, they were the only members of her family that weren't trying to kill her. Because she does not want to leave them behind, she makes them into creatures of the air.

From her first few minutes in the Convent, Mavis got the feeling that happy children are there. She has an immediate association of Merle and Pearl, the twins she lost. But there is more than this. Mavis senses, in her dreams and even waking moments, that some presence or spirit is around her. This spirit represents a danger to her; it seems to be sucking her energy and sense of well-being. Yet Mavis welcomes its interference, as if she wallows in the sense of being drained of her life force.

The creative and compassionate reader will not judge Mavis too harshly for these flights of fancy or reject her feelings outright, for they do come from somewhere. Perhaps this "succubus" is the manifestation of Mavis' guilt and shame, and her desire to be punished, just as her need to have her twins around her has resulted in her enshrining them as the Convent's angel-ghosts. There are simple answers from the field of psychology at work here. Yet we need not deny the spirituality of her experiences.

Morrison does not tell us whether the twins or the other noncorporeal figures are simply figments of Mavis's imagination, or whether we, as observers, should believe that they exist.

Study Questions

1. What made Consolata's violent illness as a child almost pleasant?

2. How much time passed between the first time Connie saw "the living man" and the next time?

3. What errand brought the man out to the Convent?

4. What particular detail about Deek did Connie notice and love?

5. What had Sister Roberta most particularly warned the Native American girls against?

6. According to Consolata's memory, over how many years had these women come to the convent?

7. How many children had Mary Magna "rescued" from the streets in South America?

8. Where had Mary Magna's non-rescued children ended up?

9. According to the narrative voice, how rare are Catholic churches and schools in Oklahoma?

10. With what arrangements had Connie tried to tempt her lover to visit her?

Answers

1. The experience of seeing a woman's face bent over hers, expressing love and worry through lake-blue eyes made Consolata's violent illness as a child almost pleasant.

2. Two months passed between the first time Connie saw "the living man" and the next time.

3. The man came out to the Convent because he wanted to buy some of its well-known peppers.

4. Connie noticed and loved Deek's smell.

5. Sister Roberta particularly warned the Native American girls against "drift."

6. According to Consolata's memory, these women had come to the convent over a period of eight years.

7. Mary Magna had "rescued" three children from the streets in South America.

8. The other children ended up in an orphanage in South America instead of coming back to Oklahoma with the nuns.

9. Catholic churches and schools in Oklahoma are "as rare as fish pockets."

10. Connie tried to tempt her lover to visit her by promising him wine, roses, peaches, and candles.

Suggested Essay Topics

1. Why would it be easier for Consolata to change life in the Convent than it would be for Deacon, Steward, Richard Misner, or anyone one else to do the same kind of things in Ruby? Try to explain exactly what Consolata does, and try to imagine how someone might do something similar in Ruby.

2. Why do you think the women in the Convent would be willing to listen to Consolata? Describe her teachings, especially the creation of the templates. What do you think was the point of that exercise? What would the women stand to gain or lose by listening to her?

Chapter Eight: Lone

Summary

Lone DuPres is hurrying back from the Convent, driving too quickly at night. One of the oldest residents in Ruby, she was rescued by the first settlers of Haven. Lone was adopted and trained by Fairy DuPres, Haven's midwife. When Fairy died, Lone took over as Ruby's midwife. Except for her, the town of Ruby is unaware of the plan cooked up by a few men to "deal with" the "threat" of the Convent women.

As she drives, Lone broods over history. Her career as a midwife is practically over. This bothers Lone, partially because it is only now that she is as mobile as she has long wanted to be, with a real car instead of recalcitrant mules or horses. But modern ideas have made women think that a hospital is the right place to have a baby, and all of Lone's traditional practices provoke scorn or amusement instead of the respect they should.

Lone remembers Fairy's comments on how their trade is truly perceived by the male half of Ruby. The husbands distrust midwives because of the unusual position in which the men are placed during their wives' childbirth. There is nothing the men can contribute to the situation, and this makes the men feel powerless, a

situation they cannot possibly deal comfortably with. This intense dislike of the situation carries over, to some extent, into distrust for the midwives themselves.

Lone's thoughts turn to the Convent again, and to the town's feelings about it. As she runs through the townsmen's problems with the Convent, she remembers the buzzards that circled near the town when K. D. and Arnette got married. When some people went to investigate, they found a car with three bodies in it, two adults and a baby, curled up peacefully. The car was near the Convent. It made the people shudder, as if those unfortunates had been a sacrifice. (The reader knows that the lost people, from the fourth chapter, were simply stubborn and ignorant, refusing to take the weather seriously and spend time in Ruby.) But no one in Ruby will take the time to understand the story of these people, because the only explanation that occurs to them fits with their prejudices.

Then it's back to the present. Looking for a special herb at night, Lone happened to be near the Oven when the nine men were there. Once they shooed away the young ones, the men sat and talked about the Convent, so as to prove what a wicked place it was. The men, outraged about what they thought the women were doing and what they saw as a threat, felt justified that violence was necessary, that their cause was righteous; they would be removing evil.

Lone stopped to listen to them, disgusted with their holier-than-thou bitterness; the reader gets to hear what the men say. We have heard the stories they tell, but in most cases we know a complete truth instead of only the dubious parts and interpretations of them.

Lone immediately goes to warn the Convent women themselves, but they do not take her warnings seriously. She then seeks help in town, for she knows that most everyone in Ruby would see this as a deeply wrong act. Yet once again, Lone is not taken seriously by some of her neighbors, except for Soane and Dovey Morgan. Lone's relatives, whom she knows will believe her, live out on the far margins of Ruby, and she heads there, knowing that she does not have much time.

By this point, the men have left the Oven and are near the Convent. They park at a distance, so as to approach silently. The mist is thick, but the sun is almost rising now. The men approach the house boldly, shooting their way through the door and then killing the first woman they see, the white girl. The other women, who were preparing food, scatter at the sound of gunfire. The men split into pairs or threes and begin to search the building. The fresh food on the great pantry table tells the men that the women were just there. The men let their guard down for a moment, and the women are upon them.

Considering that they do not have guns, the women defend themselves very well. This is the part of the raid story that the first chapter left out. The men are clubbed, scalded, and stabbed as they chase the women through the Convent's larger rooms. None of the men are killed.

The noise of conflict wakes Consolata, who first checks on Pallas' baby. Realizing that something is wrong, she explores and finds the men's first victim. In trying to comfort her, Consolata gets blood on her cheek. A few moments later, when she tries to stop the men, Deacon sees the blood, and it takes his breath away; he will never know why the blood was there, but most likely he assumed the worst. Connie is shot in the head in cold blood. The question is, by whom? Soane and Dovey, who are some distance away, disagree about who shot Connie. Each of them needs to believe that it was not her husband.

Soon after the killings, more people from Ruby arrive at the Convent. Most of them are there because they were alerted by Lone and her relatives. They have come to try and prevent what has already happened. Others will come later. For now, the morning air resounds with voices raised in loud accusations, demands for explanations, and excuses. It is believed, loudly, that the raiders have brought shame and ruin upon their families and the entire town. The censure and contempt is obvious and damning. Many relationships, including that of Soane and Dovey, change instantly and permanently.

Roger Best arrives at the Convent from an errand; he is there in his official capacity as undertaker. He is given directions about where to find the bodies, but he does not find them.

Analysis

In each case, there are reasonable explanations for the details that the men bring up around the Oven. But the men are not interested in trying to understand, just as they have never questioned their views of the world before. It is partly their rugged confidence, which is the hallmark of the American Cowboy, and also partly the sin of pride that they inherited from their parents, and imposed, or tried to impose, on their children.

We learn about each of the men, and what he has to gain by opposing the Convent women. Sargeant Person has been renting fields from Connie—with the women gone, he can make more of a profit. Menus Jury carries inside him the shameful memories of their help when he went to the Convent to detox. Wisdom Poole is upset over the fighting between his sons, Apollo and Brood. Arnold and Jeff Fleetwood carry the grief of babies who will never run and shout with joy.

Perhaps the saddest case is that of Deacon Morgan. What the invisible narrator fills in (for Lone herself would have no way of knowing this) is the way that Deacon's spirit had retreated from, and actually reversed itself from, the feelings of openness and warmth he had for Connie. Having decided that she represented a grave threat to his way of life, his heart has hardened in its efforts at self-preservation. The pendulum of his emotions swung back.

We find out that Deek knew about Soane's miscarriage and blames it on the Convent. He suspects the tea mixes that Soane gets from the Convent. He has twisted his image of Connie around to suit the impotent rage he feels about his affair with her and his betrayal of the rules that govern Ruby. For some time, he had been mightily preoccupied by the concern that Connie would have gotten pregnant and had a "mixed-up" baby, thus watering down the 8-Rock blood that made Ruby what it was. Yet his rage over this is only part of his greater sorrows, which have to do with his dead sons, the gradual fall of Ruby, and his own inability to halt either catastrophe.

Through Lone's eyes, we see beyond the rhetoric the men use to galvanize themselves into action. Each of the men has his own set of motivations for getting rid of the women, but even beyond their personal motivations, the men wish to rid their town of its troubles, and this seems like a good way. It is easier for the men to point fingers at the Convent and blame their town's ills on the women there, than it is for them to honestly examine other factors that may have led to the current problems. Having survived all of the difficulties and misfortunes of their long past, the men might very well feel that they themselves cannot be the cause of their own problems, that the origins must lie elsewhere. Women who are independent, who lie outside their standard family format, are suspect.

This goes back to Pat's realization that in order to maintain what they saw as the traditions of their elders, the men of Ruby would have to control the lives of the town's women, for they are the ones who bear the (hopefully) 8-Rock babies. The Convent women cannot be controlled. In addition to all the harm they do by distracting the town's young men, like K. D., they might provide the girls and young women of the town with an alternative, an example of choice. This is the biggest danger those women pose to the men's idea of what the town should be. For that reason alone, the women's presence is unbearable to them.

We could ask ourselves, "how was Gigi able to get a bus to make a stop in Ruby and drop her there?" Given the fact that we see no evidence that she practices witchcraft, the likeliest explanation is that she persuaded the bus driver (through flattery, bribery, or perhaps even stronger means) to deviate from his or her standard route.

In this chapter, the Oven slips to one side. As we saw in the first chapter, the Oven is the symbol of the town, a monument to all of the lives and sacrifices that went into the making of Ruby, and of Haven before it. Now the ground underneath is undermined. The new instability of the Oven is a clear, physically obvious confirmation of what the reader has known for some time—that the community of Ruby is in grave danger, and may actually be coming apart.

As before, it does not make sense that the Oven's movement is simply the result of soil erosion and falling water and has no greater significance. The Oven's instability on this night is not a mere coincidence. Morrison is quite clearly drawing a symbolic connection—the shifting of the Oven, which suggests that it may start to fall apart, is indicative of something fundamentally wrong in Ruby. The reader has known this for some time, but here is evidence and proof, something that no one in Ruby can ignore or blame on the Convent women.

As well as delineating the final step of Ruby's decline from the greatness with which it started, Morrison is also touching on a great and deep theme in twentieth-century literature. Whether or not the Oven is literally at the geographic center of the town, it is the symbolic center. In one of his best-known poems, "The Second Coming," William Butler Yeats wrote, "Things fall apart; the center cannot hold." This was his vision of the future, and it is a vision shared by many who came after him. A seminal novel by the Nigerian novelist Chinua Achebe, *Things Fall Apart*, is also part of this tradition.

Although the novel does not specifically say this, it is logical to assume that Ruby was built around the Oven, which would naturally be in the center of the town. Whether or not the town was literally built around the Oven (the novel never specifies this), it is clear that as the town's symbol falls, so does the town itself.

Now we are back to the very first sentence of the novel; the first of the women that the men kill is white. Morrison never tells the reader who the white woman is; in fact, she never actually names the race of any of the Convent women. A comment at the end of the first chapter tells us that some of the women are black, and we know that Consolata has cinnamon-colored skin, but we are never given any specifics.

This is highly significant, and develops one of the several very deep themes of the novel; Morrison has told interviewers that although race is not necessarily a large part of an individual's personality, it carries a lot of baggage in terms of how other people react to that individual. In other words, the knowledge of a person's race doesn't tell us anything about the person, but as soon as we know it, we make up our minds about who that person is. Therefore, Morrison declines to let us take an easy way out in terms of how we assess these female characters.

Readers can come up with their own personal theories about which character is white, but in the end we cannot be certain. Morrison avoided telling which woman is different from the others, so the reader is unable to think about any one of the women in a different way from the others—despite the race of any one of them, they are all equal. This is important in a novel where race is equated with identity. The Convent women themselves do not treat each other differently because of race.

The violence against the Convent women is many things at once, but most of all it is an act against something tangible. Most of the forces that threaten Ruby are invisible, and therefore largely unfightable. The inability to combat them might well so frustrate the citizens that any opportunity to actually do something concrete to help their town will be seized upon with astonishing force and determination.

Until the very end of the chapter, it would seem clear that Ruby is already doomed; the novel does not show any solutions to the problems that beset the community. The circumstances that brought Ruby and Haven into the world no longer exist, and the characters do not know how to deal with the present situation.

Study Questions

1. What was written on the sign that Lone almost knocked down?

2. What kind of herb was Lone searching for near the Oven?

3. How old is Lone in the present?

4. Do the men go anywhere after leaving the Oven and before going to the Convent?

5. Whom does Lone seek out once she gets her car out of the ditch?

6. What time did the Convent women wake to prepare for the day?

7. Who shoots the white woman?

8. About whom did Dovey Morgan once have a strange, portentous dream?

9. Who took the knife out of Menus Jury's shoulder?

10. When Roger Best goes out to the Convent, what is he unable to find?

Answers

1. "Early Melones" was written on the sign that Lone almost knocked down.

2. Lone was searching for a mandrake root in the stream bed near the Oven.

3. Lone is 86.

4. Yes. To avoid the rain, the men go to the shed behind Sargeant Person's barn.

5. Once she gets her car out of the ditch, Lone seeks out Pious DuPres.

6. The Convent women woke at 4:00 a.m. to prepare for the day.

7. Steward Morgan shoots the white woman.

8. Dovey Morgan once had a strange, portentous dream about the man she called "Friend." In the dream she washed his hair and then woke up to find her hands wet with suds.

9. Reverend Pulliam took the knife out of Menus Jury's shoulder.

10. When Roger Best goes out to the Convent, he cannot find any evidence that anything unusual took place there. He cannot find any of the bodies, any blood, or the Cadillac that Mavis had brought.

Suggested Essay Topics

1. This chapter might be the most intense part of the novel. What were your feelings as you read this chapter? What parts of the chapter had the greatest effect on you? Why those parts?

2. Based on the entire novel, but most of all on how we see the twins in this chapter, which of the brothers is the stronger man?

Chapter Nine: Save-Marie

New Characters:

Save-Marie: *not a true character; she has died just before the time frame of the chapter. She was the youngest of Jeff and Sweetie Fleetwood's sickly children. The others are Noah, Esther, and Ming.*

Manley Gibson: *Gigi's father, a convict recently removed from death row.*

Dee Dee Truelove: *Pallas' mother.*

Summary

This chapter opens with a funeral, the first one in Ruby's history. Save-Marie was the youngest of Jeff and Sweetie's children, all of whom, we will recall, were extremely unhealthy from their first breaths. Save-Marie's funeral is the first public one in Ruby, and she is considered to be the first citizen of Ruby to die in the town; although Delia Best, Pat's mother, is buried in her own "back yard," her death was not thought of as official, for several reasons. Regardless of this, the aura of immortality that Pat had once thought about is gone. Some speculate, privately, that the mysterious veil of protection is gone because of what happened at the Convent.

That was in July, and now it is November. The funeral is well attended, but Sweetie refuses to be consoled. She harbors much bitterness toward the Morgan brothers. Some, notably Pat Best, speculate about whether or not Sweetie's reserve has in it elements of manipulation. Always the observer, Pat considers "the new" Ruby and thinks about the Oven. There is new graffiti there, and it reads "We Are the Furrow of His Brow."

Even several months after the incident at the Convent, the town talks of little else. It took a little while for the town to realize that "the law," which they expected to seize them even though it had never done so before, did not see what they had done. They would not be taken to jail for their acts of killing.

By disposing of the bodies and the car, Lone DuPres has seen to it that the law would not descend upon the citizens of Ruby. Lone

feels that the opportunity to rescue the town had nothing to do with any generosity on her part but was part of God's plan for Ruby. She wonders if the townspeople will see the obvious sign of God's favor in this spectacular rescue. They don't. The freedom from consequence simply makes them more sure of themselves and more cocky.

Lone, who more than anyone else had been an eyewitness to the men's planning, has become upset by the shameless way in which the men and their families quietly accuse each other while trying to downplay the incident into nonexistence. She tells what she knows, but no one is interested in doing any kind of investigation. When they saw that they had gotten away with what they had done, the men involved (with the assistance of their families and friends) created different explanations and stories about what did or did not happen that morning. The stories, which increase certain tensions in the town, are designed to downplay the teller's role in the whole thing. They serve to cloud the subject and make getting to the truth (which no one really wants to do anyway) almost impossible.

The lives of the men who attacked the Convent are explored. At the funeral are Harper Jury and Sargeant Person, both looking as proud as if they had not so much as a single sin to confess. Nearby is K. D., more contrite. He and Arnette are expecting their second child, and Steward has taken them under his wing; he will make them rich.

But most changed of all is Deacon Morgan. A single moment has divorced him not only from the town but from his own brother as well. Deacon wonders about what Connie was saying before she was shot. "You're back," she had said. At first, he had thought that she was referring to him, but later on he was not so sure. Now he knows that he will never know what she meant, and he feels that Steward shot Connie before anyone, especially Deacon, could learn the meaning of her words.

When Deacon wanted to unburden himself, he went to Richard Misner to talk, though he has never needed to do this before. He walks to Misner's house barefoot, past the trees that he had helped to plant. Some neighbors, and the curious in general, marveled to see him walking barefoot. Deacon thinks about the evening six years ago, when he, Steward, and K. D. had met there to go to the Fleetwood's home. Back then Deacon, like his brother, was arrogant and unbendingly prideful. Such is not the case now.

Deacon tells Misner many things, including a story about Zechariah Morgan. It turns out that, long ago, Zechariah had a twin brother; just as Zechariah himself had been known as "Coffee," the brother's name was "Tea." It happened that, just before the group was set to leave what had been their homes, a group of racist whites demanded that the brothers dance for them. Zechariah's refusal resulted in his getting shot in the foot. The sight of seeing his brother promptly begin to dance changed Zechariah deeply; the brothers parted, and Tea never joined the group of settlers that founded Haven. Zechariah never spoke of his brother again. Now Deacon can understand such feelings, although Misner counsels him to avoid the hard heart of pride.

More than anyone else, Richard Misner and Anna Flood do want to make sense of what happened. They were not in Ruby at the time of the raid. When they returned, two days later, and heard the different versions of the story, they decided to go to the Convent to find out for themselves.

At the Convent, they find not only the floor murals that the women drew but something more. They describe it as a window, or a door, though it does not physically exist. Although they recognize that it is something beyond their frame of reference, something they could not possibly understand, they are not afraid of it. Yet they do not take the time to investigate what they have glimpsed and speak of it later in a joking, almost lighthearted fashion.

The funeral service is ending. Billie Delia, who is there out of a sense of obligation, steps away for some private time. Like her mother, Pat Best, Billie sees through the town's arrangements of history and power and control. She considers life in Ruby and thinks about the Convent women, who were very important people in her life, like role models. She hopes that they are out there somewhere, still somehow enjoying themselves, and making themselves into who they want to be.

Gigi appears before her father, Manley Gibson, whose prison sentence was just reduced from the death penalty to life imprisonment. He is delighted to see her, and they talk briefly. He notices her shaved head and military gear. Later, Gigi strips naked and swims with an unnamed companion.

Dee Dee Truelove, a painter, spots her daughter Pallas, who crosses the street outside. She seems to be carrying a sword and is imbued with light. Later, Pallas comes inside to retrieve an old pair of sandals. Mother and daughter never speak to each other.

Sally Albright is on break from work when she sees her mother in a coffee shop. Sally is almost overwhelmed to be sitting with her mother after all this time. Mavis is distracted by how good all the food tastes. The two sit and talk about Sal's brothers and the past; they have a very healing encounter, especially Sal, but it is too brief. Becoming emotional, she asks for forgiveness, which Mavis gives effortlessly and lightheartedly, putting the past to rest.

A woman named Jean has been looking for Seneca for years. In crowds at concerts and shopping malls, she seeks her constantly. Finally, at a rock concert, she sees and talks briefly with Seneca, who does not seem to know her. Their conversation is quite brief, mostly because Jack, Jean's husband, is impatient to leave. Jean never wanted Jack to know that she had a child when she was 14 years old. Even Seneca had thought that Jean was her sister.

The final scene is set on a beach. Two women sit there, watching ships full of pilgrims arrive. One woman is bent down into the other woman's lap; the woman is stroking her hair. The pilgrims, exhausted and brokenhearted, are searching for paradise.

Analysis

This chapter holds mystery, as had others before it. Lone is left alone at the scene of the massacre, yet Roger Best finds nothing there. The job of "cleaning up" could not have been an easy task for an old woman acting alone. How she does it is never revealed, and we do not know for sure that she had anything to do with the disappearances of the bodies, blood, and car. This is another mystery, and one of the most powerful in the entire novel.

Ever since the Morgan brothers brought their sister Ruby home from the hospital, where she died on a bench, there has not been a single death in town. That was over 20 years ago, but now things are different. Pat Best realizes that Sweetie's stubbornness about her infant daughter's burial will oblige the 8-Rocks that run Ruby

to open an official cemetery, which will inevitably signify something profound about their loss of control over their world. Now that someone has died in the town of Ruby, there will probably be more deaths. Paradise has been lost.

As we have seen before, this change in the way things are is not something that the reader can reasonably pass off as coincidence. After no deaths for so long, the fact that this happened after the raid on the Convent is crucially important. This is the stuff of fairy tales, as opposed to the historical narrative found elsewhere in the novel. As has been noted before, it is this grand scale, reminiscent of mythology, that distinguishes Toni Morrison's novels from those of other contemporary American writers.

Of all the mysteries, especially mysticism-based mysteries, in the novel, this business of the window or door or "portal" is one of the strangest. Rather than trying to come up with a definitive answer, let us deal with what we know for certain. Except for the men who came to raid the Convent, and then Roger Best, no one from Ruby ever went into the cellar, and so none of them saw what was down there. The men themselves had other things on their minds. In fact, none of the other characters ever commented on any such object.

But what about the women who lived there? They never talked about a portal, but this proves nothing. Perhaps the women saw but never spoke of it. Perhaps all the changes and healing that the women went through were possible because of the portal, and they took it as a given, and not worth mentioning.

But Richard and Anna did see something. It is unlikely that they were hallucinating. What exactly did they see? The text seems to suggest that, just as a door or window can provide a vista of a different landscape, this portal represents an alternative. It is found at the heart of this special building, in which several fractured lives were mended. It is the essence of a healing place, a spot near the templates in which the Convent women rediscovered their selves and were reborn.

As with the other mystical parts of this novel, this material can be difficult. Yet we should remember that, time and again, this novel has shown us logical explanations for seemingly unnatural things. Therefore, we might well consider that Anna and Richard were perceiving the essence of the place, that it represented a choice for the women who lived there. We might even say that they saw the physical manifestation of choice itself. Maybe the window/door simply means freedom and a chance to go someplace and be someone else.

More interesting than, "what did they see?" is "how is it that they were the ones who saw it?," or "why did they respond the way they did?" Perhaps they saw what they did because of who they are. They are clearly the most sympathetic people in Ruby. As we could tell from the first time we saw them together, in "Seneca," they are the only two characters in the entire novel who are in love, and, unlike most of their neighbors, they are constantly thinking about specific and constructive ways to help their community. Whereas other characters seem concerned only about their personal situations, Richard and Anna have a larger vision.

All of this means that they are open to seeing and feeling things that others from Ruby would miss. But why weren't they frightened, and why didn't they investigate what they saw? Weren't they curious?

After the funeral service and all the tangents that the narrator explores, we are done with the story of Ruby. Questions remain, of course, the biggest ones being, "what happens now? What will their future be like?" We can speculate on our own, but we are not told. Yet the book is not over.

The second part of the chapter is a series of vignettes that, like the first half of the second chapter, might at first seem completely unrelated to the main story. But of course they are related. The little series of interactions concern people from the earlier parts of the lives of the Convent women. These people have a chance to see and talk with those women, who we saw die in the previous chapter.

But when we look more closely, we see that the vignettes concern not the women themselves, but characters who have "wronged" the four women. The appearance of Gigi, Mavis, Pallas, and Seneca in each of these scenes allows Manley, Sally, Dee Dee, and Jean to express their regret for what they had done. Although the expression of regret does not necessarily result in a reconciliation (only Sally seems to be totally forgiven), there is one thing all four of these people take from their meetings. It seems that due to their visitations, the family characters will all learn from their past mistakes, a marked contrast to how the Rubyites treat their past.

Jean's meeting with Seneca was painful, but as Seneca mentions, "everyone makes mistakes." Jean, Manley, and Dee Dee cannot have their daughters back, but can take some solace in the knowledge that their daughters exist, whether physically or spiritually. The lessons that the women of the Convent seem to teach is that it is all right to acknowledge and learn from the mistakes of the past in order to grow spiritually.

Although there is no earthly justice or retribution for the women, their spirits have better things to do than haunt or hound their killers. They get a sense of peace (and in the process they might make the reader feel a little better, after the brutality of their deaths) by visiting people from their pasts. Most of those visited have many questions, but these remain unanswered. The Convent's women are still mysterious: we do not even know for certain that they were killed, even though some of Ruby's men said so. The women's futures are left hanging.

The thread of mystery that runs throughout this novel has become actual mysticism on occasion and does so again at the end. We knew something about Consolata's spiritual teachings and the business of her supposedly raising the dead. But Morrison moves beyond these concerns, into something still more vague.

At its very heart, Paradise is a tragedy, in the same way that Greek drama or some of Shakespeare's plays are tragedies. The two communities are doomed. The fact that men from Ruby feel they have to attack the Convent shows how desperate they are to do something to rescue their home and people from the forces of destruction. The wars these characters have had to wage in order to achieve their paradise have made them into fighters. Paradise must be fought for; when it comes to fighting for a place, simple variables apply. How many people are fighting together, how much experience they have in fighting, and who gets to the battlefield first, all determine victory.

But how tragic that this is the case. No one in the book could stay peaceful in their paradise. Can we live in a world where paradise is a possibility?

One thing is certain. So long as race and class are divisive parts of the human experience, paradise will remain only a dream.

Study Questions

1. What had Sweetie refused to discuss?

2. How was Esther, Jeff and Sweetie's second child, given her name?

3. What didn't Pat Best tell Richard?

4. Who wept before the entire congregation of the Holy Redeemer?

5. Where do the Carys live, and how do we know this?

6. What was the first question that Manley Gibson asked his daughter, Gigi?

7. What part of Pallas did Dee Dee Truelove feel she had been unable to capture in the many portraits she had painted?

8. What does Mavis do when Sally hugs her tightly?

9. How does Seneca's friend clean the wounds on Seneca's hands?

10. What is the last word of this novel?

Answers

1. Sweetie Fleetwood refused to discuss the burial of her daughter Save-Marie. Sweetie was unwilling to have her baby girl buried on Morgan-owned land.

2. Esther was named after her grandmother, who had taken such good care of Noah, her older brother.

3. Pat Best did not tell Richard her version of the Convent raid: that nine 8-Rock men brutally murdered the Convent women because those women were deemed "impure temptresses," and because the men thought that they would get away with the murders.

4. Wisdom Poole wept before the entire congregation of the Holy Redeemer.

5. The Carys (including Reverend Cary) live on Cross Mark. We know this because Lily Cary calls out to Deacon Morgan from her porch.

6. Manley Gibson asked Gigi if she heard that he had been paroled from death row.

7. Dee Dee Truelove had trouble capturing different parts of Pallas's face and body in the many portraits she painted.

8. Mavis groans slightly and laughs when Sally hugs her tightly. She tells her daughter that she's "a little sore on that side."

9. Seneca's friend cleans the wounds on Seneca's hands by pouring beer on them.

10. The last word of this novel is "Paradise."

Suggested Essay Topics

1. How would you explain the phenomenon at the Convent? Do you think Lone removed all evidence of the massacre? What other explanations could there be? If Lone did remove the bodies, blood, and car, do you think it was the right thing to do? Why or why not? What would you have done if you were in her situation, and why?

2. Why do you think Sweetie felt the way she did about the Morgan brothers? What different kinds of harm had they done, if any? How would you feel, and what would you do, if you were Sweetie, or another member of the Fleetwood family?

Sample Analytical Paper Topics

Topic #1

Compare the hardships that beset the original founders of Haven with the hardships and stresses of the citizens of Ruby.

Outline

I.   Thesis Statement: *The people who founded Haven had to endure different hardships and were under different stresses than the citizens of Ruby.*

   A.   The founders of Haven had particular stresses and hardships.

   B.   The founders of Ruby had particular stresses and hardships.

II.   The founders of Haven worked together.

   A.   They left the same homes, together, for similar reasons.

   B.   They were under the same stresses, like survival.

   C.   They were already in the same families.

   D.   They had to pool their resources in order to make it through the lean times.

III.   The citizens of Ruby have not been working together.

   A.   They compete with one another.

    B.   They have religious differences.

    C.   There are more people in total, and larger groups are always harder to manage.

    D.   They do not always wish each other well.

IV. The past weighs on the current population of Ruby.

    A.   The Morgan brothers are constantly concerned with what their ancestors would think.

    B.   Many people are unwilling to talk about their family's history.

    C.   New ideas are suspect, and people have little curiosity about the outside world.

    D.   The pressures of the past hamper people's current freedom.

Topic #2

Perspective: Rights exist only so long as someone else does not deny them.

Outline

I. Thesis Statement: *In the battle between the people of Ruby and the women in the Convent, each side has a right to its existence. But one group has more rights than the other. Conflicts occur when one group puts its rights first.*

    A.   The political status of the men of Ruby.

    B.   The political status of the women of Ruby.

    C.   The political status of the Convent women.

II. The people of Ruby have more rights.

    A.   They arrived first.

    B.   Their ancestors taught them how to live.

    C.   The general countryside is hostile.

    D.   The Rubyites built their town from practically nothing, and they own their land.

III.   The women of the Convent have rights.

    A.   They have no people who love them.

    B.   No one from Ruby has ever had to fight for survival, but all of the Convent women have had to fight.

    C.   The general countryside is hostile.

    D.   The women have fled their previous lives, and they deserve peace.

IV.   Neither group has a greater right.

    A.   Each side had equal rights; they could have lived together.

    B.   Each side should have sat down and discussed the situation.

    C.   One of the groups should have tried alternatives.

Topic #3

Pick three characters you like or dislike the most. Compare and contrast them in emotional, moral, and political terms.

Outline

I.   Connie/Consolata

    A.   Her past has made her a powerful loner.

    B.   She is a great teacher and leader.

    C.   She can be harsh with others.

    D.   She has been very lonely.

II.   Mavis Albright

    A.   She is a bad woman—she let her children die.

    B.   She is a good woman—she has shown much compassion for others.

    C.   She does not like Gigi.

    D.   She is a confusing, contradictory character.

III.   Richard Misner

    A.   He is a kind man, always trying to help others.

B. He is a wise and visionary person, managing to see beyond the petty little world of Ruby.

C. He is a naive fool, trying to mess with a working community.

D. He should/should not stay in Ruby.

SECTION FOUR

Bibliography

Century, Douglas. *Toni Morrison: Black Americans of Achievement.* New York: Chelsea House Publishers, 1994.

Durham, Philip, and Everett L. Jones. *The Negro Cowboys.* New York: Dodd, Mead & Company, 1965.

Katz, William Loren. *The Black West.* New York: Simon and Schuster, 1996.

Love, Nat. *The Life and Adventures of Nat Love.* Baltimore: Black Classics Press, 1988.

White, Richard. *A New History of the American West.* Norman: University of Oklahoma Press, 1991.

MAXnotes®

REA's Literature Study Guides

MAXnotes® are student-friendly. They offer a fresh look at masterpieces of literature, presented in a lively and interesting fashion. **MAXnotes®** offer the essentials of what you should know about the work, including outlines, explanations and discussions of the plot, character lists, analyses, and historical context. **MAXnotes®** are designed to help you think independently about literary works by raising various issues and thought-provoking ideas and questions. Written by literary experts who currently teach the subject, **MAXnotes®** enhance your understanding and enjoyment of the work.

Available **MAXnotes®** include the following:

Absalom, Absalom!	Henry IV, Part I	Othello
The Aeneid of Virgil	Henry V	Paradise
Animal Farm	The House on Mango Street	Paradise Lost
Antony and Cleopatra	Huckleberry Finn	A Passage to India
As I Lay Dying	I Know Why the Caged	Plato's Republic
As You Like It	Bird Sings	Portrait of a Lady
The Autobiography of	The Iliad	A Portrait of the Artist
Malcolm X	Invisible Man	as a Young Man
The Awakening	Jane Eyre	Pride and Prejudice
Beloved	Jazz	A Raisin in the Sun
Beowulf	The Joy Luck Club	Richard II
Billy Budd	Jude the Obscure	Romeo and Juliet
The Bluest Eye, A Novel	Julius Caesar	The Scarlet Letter
Brave New World	King Lear	Sir Gawain and the
The Canterbury Tales	Leaves of Grass	Green Knight
The Catcher in the Rye	Les Misérables	Slaughterhouse-Five
The Color Purple	Lord of the Flies	Song of Solomon
The Crucible	Macbeth	The Sound and the Fury
Death in Venice	The Merchant of Venice	The Stranger
Death of a Salesman	Metamorphoses of Ovid	Sula
The Divine Comedy I: Inferno	Metamorphosis	The Sun Also Rises
Dubliners	Middlemarch	A Tale of Two Cities
The Edible Woman	A Midsummer Night's Dream	The Taming of the Shrew
Emma	Moby-Dick	Tar Baby
Euripides' Medea & Electra	Moll Flanders	The Tempest
Frankenstein	Mrs. Dalloway	Tess of the D'Urbervilles
Gone with the Wind	Much Ado About Nothing	Their Eyes Were Watching God
The Grapes of Wrath	Mules and Men	Things Fall Apart
Great Expectations	My Antonia	To Kill a Mockingbird
The Great Gatsby	Native Son	To the Lighthouse
Gulliver's Travels	1984	Twelfth Night
Handmaid's Tale	The Odyssey	Uncle Tom's Cabin
Hamlet	Oedipus Trilogy	Waiting for Godot
Hard Times	Of Mice and Men	Wuthering Heights
Heart of Darkness	On the Road	Guide to Literary Terms

RESEARCH & EDUCATION ASSOCIATION
61 Ethel Road W. • Piscataway, New Jersey 08854
Phone: (732) 819-8880   **website: www.rea.com**

Please send me more information about MAXnotes®.

Name _____

Address _____

City _____ State _____ Zip_____